D0378987

# JOAN CHITTISTER

# Grace-filled moments WITH Sr. Joan

## 365 REFLECTIONS ON LIFE, LOSS, HEALING & JOY

**TWENTY-THIRD PUBLICATIONS**

twentythirdpublications.com

**Twenty-Third Publications**
One Montauk Avenue, Suite 200
New London, CT 06320
(860) 437-3012 or (800) 321-0411
www.twentythirdpublications.com

ISBN: 978-1-62785-642-3
Printed in the U.S.A.

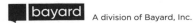

A division of Bayard, Inc.

# CONTENTS

# To Hear a Broken Heart

Sometimes the holiest messages come from the most mundane of places and just when we don't expect them. For instance, "Listening" is one of the foundations of Benedictine life. In fact, the very first word of this ancient sixth-century Rule is "Listen." "Listen carefully, my child, to my instructions...." Ho, hum. More of the same.

Until Beyoncé says it. Then suddenly we understand. Suddenly, the place of listening in life becomes crystal clear. Listening is the glue—or the downfall—of every relationship, she sings to us. If you want a New Year full of good relationships, listening is the key. Better yet, she outlines the process in straight and painful terms. She leaves no doubt where the problem lies.

She sings in "Listen" the universal cry of the lonely human spirit. She tells us the problem that attends everyone who tries to talk to us but whom we ignore. Often nicely. As in, "I'm so sorry you're going through this. I really wish I could help...."

But then comes the mention of "the very important meeting to which I really need to run," which tells the lonely person that she and her pain are not very important. Not even important enough for another twenty minutes of understanding and life—and the hope that comes when someone she values takes the time to listen to the pain. And so her heart dies. And no one notices that either.

The singer is crying out to have her own voice heard, to have her own needs recognized, to become her own person rather than the shadow of another.

When we stop listening to the other people in our lives, not only do the relationships deteriorate but we become separated from the well of Wisdom around us. No matter how together we look, we have become hopelessly separated. The problem is that in our own desire to be listened to, to be really heard and understood by another, we miss one of the basic messages of life: It's not just about me. It's about the other person, too. Anything else is not communication; it's manipulation.

Jesus listened to people. In the bonds he forged with the poor, the sick, the outcast, and the foreigner lay compassion, truth, support, and growth. First, he listened to what people were saying. Then, he cured them of what they wanted to have cured rather than what others might have decided they most needed—like faith or patience or trust.

To talk without listening to the other is simply chatting. It fills time but changes nothing. In self-centeredness, friendships end, marriages dissolve, relationships become sterile. Most of all, wisdom, holy friendship, the sharing of insights that come from experience, evaporate.

Friendship, marriage, and lifelong relationships come from listening to one another.

Clearly, when the Rule of Benedict calls for "listening," it's not calling for some kind of hollow obedience; it's calling for real relationships.

**JANUARY 1** Here's a quick test to tell us how we interact with people: What are you doing when the other person is talking? In his leadership courses, Steven R. Covey gives us a clue. "Most people," he says, "do not listen with the intent to understand; they listen with the intent to reply." And that leads where?

**JANUARY 2** The desire to have our ideas and dreams heard is the foundation of discernment. We make better decisions when we can compare our own assumptions with the experiences of others.

**JANUARY 3** People who listen to us, who help us hear ourselves and our motives without condemning us for having them, give us a chance to grow. How? By giving us the opportunity to think things through in all their dimensions from all directions.

**JANUARY 4** Asking a person to defend or justify what they haven't yet done—as in "You're going to change jobs again? That's ridiculous!"—is not communication. It is argument. And poor argument at that.

**JANUARY 5** Communication ends when I cease to hear the cry, the need, the unspoken pain of the other. "No one is as deaf," the Jewish proverb teaches, "as the one who will not listen."

**JANUARY 6** If there is any ministry on earth worth being part of it is the ministry of those who can hear a broken heart. "Fixing" a problem is a final act of mercy. Understanding it is the first.

**JANUARY 7** All the great saints bent their lives to hear the stories of the sad and the lonely, the forgotten and the accused. It is that kind of "loaves and fishes" that we are all able to give the starving. If only we will.

**JANUARY 8** The genius of holy communication lies in listening to a problem before we decide to fix it without really understanding it. Then, as Scripture says, "the last evil is worse than the first." Or as Louise von François writes, "We never listen when we are eager to speak."

**JANUARY 9** To make friends, all you need to do is to listen to them. To have a friend is to have someone who is really listening to you. "Attention," Anne-Sophie Swetchine writes, "is a tacit and continual compliment."

**JANUARY 10** Society's great, unremitting question is always, "To whom do we listen?" When was the last time we saw conferences of inner-city representatives who were invited to tell their elected representatives what it would take to make their neighborhoods peaceful, beautiful, and safe?

**JANUARY 11** It is easy to cover up unhappiness with security in "things," but the pains of the lonely and the unfulfilled wealthy are no less debilitating than the pains of the insecure and the poor.

**JANUARY 12** The technology of "global ears" has done nothing, it seems, to calm our anxieties. On the contrary. Obviously, technology connects us electronically. It does not necessarily give us anyone to really talk to.

"It seems rather incongruous," Erma Bombeck writes, "that in a society of super sophisticated communication, we often suffer from a shortage of listeners."

**JANUARY 13** Unhappiness comes with feeling abandoned, alone, unaccompanied through life. Happiness comes if one other person really cares whether we come home at night or not. "Those who are unhappy have no need for anything in this world," Simone Weil wrote, "but people capable of giving them their attention."

**JANUARY 14** Electronic contact is no guarantee of love and listening. It's just a means of finding love and care if, of course, it's really there to be had. It's important not to confuse the two. "Listening," Krista Tippett reminds us, "is about being present, not just about being quiet."

**JANUARY 15** Everyone needs someone who cares enough to hear them through, to support them as they take their next moves through life.

**JANUARY 16** Listening isn't just about helping someone else. It is also about being willing to learn from someone else. As Plutarch says, "Know how to listen and you will profit even from those who talk badly."

**JANUARY 17** When friends or couples drift apart, two things are at work. The first is that talk has taken the place of attention. The second is that distance has filled the relationship with foreign noise.

**JANUARY 18** To be a good listener, it is necessary to ask the right questions. Then, of course, we must have the patience to permit the other person to answer them.

**JANUARY 19** To feel unheard is one of life's greatest deprivations. Which is why solitary confinement can be so painful, so inhumane. Only by stretching ourselves to speak the real truth can we ever really grow beyond ourselves.

**JANUARY 20** The person who listens to the other perceives the person that cannot really be seen otherwise. "After all," George Eliot says, "the true seeing is within."

**JANUARY 21** Interruption is the enemy of friendship. It gives no chance of listening to the person within the person who is trying to be heard. It is the message of disinterest, the end of possibility.

**JANUARY 22** Relationships are not about the bond of common activities. They are made of common understanding and an uncommon depth of attention.

**JANUARY 23** Life is made up of the stories we tell and the stories we have never told. Friendship and love are fed best by the stories we have never told being told to the one who wants to receive them. "One of the most valuable things we can do to heal one another," Rebecca Falls writes, "is listen to each other's stories."

**JANUARY 24** Those who are full of themselves are always too noisy inside, too busy outside, to listen to anyone else. They are a world unto themselves whose attention is superficial and whose love satisfies only themselves. As Calvin Coolidge said, "It takes a great person to be a good listener."

**JANUARY 25** Scripture is clear about God's relationship with humans. "God hears us," the Scripture points out over and over. God is the Great Listener. It's we who must learn to listen back.

**JANUARY 26** Listening is as much a personal strength as it is a skill. Larry King explains the point when he says, "I remind myself every morning: Nothing I say this day will teach me anything. So if I'm going to learn, I must do it by listening."

**JANUARY 27** Prayer is dialogue with God, the ancients taught. We pray; God listens. The hard part comes with learning that God is talking to us too. The measure of our spiritual growth lies in whether we are willing to listen back in order to understand the real message there—or not.

**JANUARY 28**  The quality of listening depends on the degree of interest we bring to the person and the conversation at hand. It's easy to nod and look interested in someone. What is difficult is to care enough about what we hear to truly want to continue the conversation. Both for their sake and for ours.

**JANUARY 29**  When we listen to a person, we take them into our lives. We welcome them and all their concerns, all their interests, all their openness. "Listening," Henri Nouwen wrote, "is a form of spiritual hospitality by which you invite strangers to become friends."

**JANUARY 30**  There are no gifts as precious as the gifts of time and listening. They are the only real signs of care and interest, of concern and delight we have to bring to a relationship. They invite the gift of mutual self-giving. "Our listening," Rachel Naomi Remen writes, "creates a sanctuary for the homeless parts within another person."

Listening is the ear of the soul. It is alert to everything and everyone in the universe. Abel Herzberg tells the story of a rabbi who saw his son deep in prayer while in the corner stood a cradle with a crying baby. "Can't you hear the baby crying?" the rabbi asked. And the son answered, "Oh, Father, I was lost in God." But the rabbi said back, "One who is lost in God can see the very fly crawling up the wall."

FEBRUARY

# Choose Joy

The Rule of Benedict, on which the lives of multiple religious women and men have been based for over 1,500 years, was written by an Italian in sixth-century Italy. I have always been secretly happy about that.

In that era the commonplace image of a monk was still the recluse in a dry and barren desert. Benedict, however, created another kind of monasticism, of spirituality, of holiness. He presented the spiritual world with the concept of "community" as sanctifier, of "family" as a spiritual discipline. Rather than isolation from the components of life, his spirituality was about single-minded search for God, not singleness for its own sake.

To this day Benedict wants those who follow his very moderate, very profound spiritual counsel to learn to live an ordinary life extraordinarily well. Chapter 40 of the Rule of Benedict, on "The Proper Amount of Drink," demonstrates that core value with overwhelming simplicity. "We believe," he writes, "that a hemina of wine is sufficient for each." The hemina is an ancient liquid measure variously defined as between six and eight ounces.

Wine, the fruit of the vine, was basic to the Italian diet—and still is.

One thing that Italians understand better than many is that there is a difference between a spiritual life and an ascetical life. Lots of people are highly spiritual but not necessarily known for their asceticism or self-denial. St. Nicholas, the model for the modern Santa Claus, for instance, gave gifts to everyone. Jesus, too, was not averse to parties and moments of relaxation. He went to the marriage feast at Cana and multiplied the wine. He celebrated the Passover meal even at the brink of death. He used a good many dinner parties as images of life in his parables. He was criticized for it but ignored the religious pressure to suck the joy out of life. And so, you see, to this day, in Italy, there is always wine served at meal-times. And it is also served in monasteries, as well as in public restaurants and at family meals.

There are simply some things in life that are meant to be enjoyed. There is something about joy, this monastic rule affirms, that is as holy as suffering can ever be. There is an asceticism that leads to sourness of attitudes, to negative judgments of normal and healthy things, as in, "You mean she's going to take a day off when she could get paid for working overtime?" Or, better yet, "You mean that priests golf and sisters swim and religious communities do yoga?"

Genuinely holy people know that life is to be enjoyed as well as disciplined, happy as well as controlled, full of the juice of life as well as stripped of good times in the name of holiness. Why? Because joy is hardwired into the human condition. More, we are meant to be joyful because life itself is good and also to be enjoyed.

The wholesale attack on enjoyment of any kind came out of a period of time when avid extremists taught that the body was bad, humor was decadent, friends were a frivolous distraction, and partaking of the fruit of the vine was a sin against sanctity. The body, that group insisted, was evil, bad, the site of sin. And that kind of holiness the church declared to be heresy.

Good for us. The philosophy of "extremism in nothing; moderation in all things" claimed the day. And it should. Because if truth were known, moderation is far more difficult to achieve and follow than extremism in either direction. As Augustine of Hippo said, "To many, total abstinence is easier than perfect moderation."

**FEBRUARY 1** The world does not need any more sad saints. We need hope and faith and joy. Life is difficult enough without making up austerity games to prove how happy we are with misery.

**FEBRUARY 2** No, life is not one long party. That's exactly why parties are so important. They remind us of God's eternal goodness. They help us to remember on difficult days that the sun of the heart will surely rise again for us.

**FEBRUARY 3** The "attitude of gratitude"—appreciation for the small goods of life: the taste of warm, fresh bread, the birthday card in the mailbox, the hour of quiet that returns us to ourselves—is itself a spiritual exercise. It stops us from becoming whiners. It keeps us in touch with the goodness of God.

**FEBRUARY 4** Gratitude for small things helps us to see life from a more realistic perspective. Great, great joys are rare in life. It's learning to recognize the small gifts in our lives that gives us deep, but often overlooked, constant joy. As Jean Webster puts it, "It isn't the great big pleasures that count the most; it's making a great deal out of the little ones."

**FEBRUARY 5** Joy is an impulse within us, not simply a temporary reaction to something outside of us. Joyfulness is a state of mind that can either be ignored—as in "bah, humbug"—or cultivated—as in the personal decision to have a merry Christmas or a happy birthday or a great day in the hammock reading a good book. It's all our own choice.

**FEBRUARY 6** When we take joy out of life we take God out of our lives. We choose to be dour—and it affects everyone we touch. E.B. White writes, "I arise in the morning torn between a desire to improve the world and a desire to enjoy the world." The answer, of course, is that we must do both.

**FEBRUARY 7** Pleasure cultivates joy, but it is no substitute for it. Otherwise, when the momentary pleasure ends so shall the joy. As Søren Kierkegaard says, "Many of us pursue pleasure with such breathless haste that we hurry past it."

**FEBRUARY 8** When joy suffuses us, shines out of every pore, we spark the search for joy in others. We remind people to reignite the flame of deep happiness within themselves before it is too sparse to mine again.

**FEBRUARY 9** Some people aren't happy unless they're unhappy. Beware. Negativity is an infectious disease. Find someone else with whom to enjoy life before you lose your own.

**FEBRUARY 10** Celebration is the light of life. As long as we have things to celebrate, there will be a reason to get up on the mornings in between. "Celebration," Corita Kent said, "is a kind of food we all need in our lives. Each individual brings a special recipe or offering to it, so that together we will make a great feast. Celebration is a human need that we must not, and cannot, deny."

**FEBRUARY 11** Meaningless asceticism, giving things up just to give something up and calling the denial holiness, is a kind of empty pain. Asceticism is meant to give us something we need—patience, perdurance, health, for instance—not something that simply aggravates our souls, like hair shirts and thistles.

**FEBRUARY 12** So much negative asceticism or pseudo-holiness only makes us worse as human beings. Lin-Chi the Chinese sage wrote, "When hungry, eat your rice; when tired, close your eyes. Fools may laugh at me, but the wise know what I mean."

**FEBRUARY 13** Life's burdens will come soon enough—and often. There is no need to make them up. The need is to deal with them well, joyfully, or at least patiently aware that on the other side of pain is great new life again.

**FEBRUARY 14** Moderation is the key to happiness. "It is not the one who has too little," Seneca says, "but the one who always craves more, who is poor."

**FEBRUARY 15** Moderation saves us from the excesses that destroy us. "If one oversteps the bounds of moderation," the philosopher Epictetus writes, "the greatest pleasures cease to please." Or to put it another way: too much of the best of ice cream, however good, will make a person sick.

**FEBRUARY 16** The purpose of asceticism is not deprivation of the good. Asceticism, the ability to say "enough," leaves us with space for new joy.

**FEBRUARY 17** Being able to let go of something is the best proof we have that we can. As the old comedy routine goes, "I can stop drinking anytime I want to. I've already done it a hundred times." Or as Ali ibn Ali Talib says, "Asceticism is not that you should not own anything, but that nothing should own you."

**FEBRUARY 18** There is joy in letting go of excess. It frees us from yesterday so that we can begin to explore a new tomorrow.

**FEBRUARY 19** To take joy in something new freshens the soul. It lifts us out of the routine of old questions and opens the mind to new possibilities. As Ovid says, "A field that has rested gives a bountiful crop."

**FEBRUARY 20** When we find ourselves sitting around waiting for something good to happen to us, it is a very bad sign. The fact is that life requires that we make good things happen to us by developing them ourselves. "Living well," Maya Angelou writes, "is an art that can be developed: a love of life and ability to take great pleasure from small offerings."

**FEBRUARY 21** Even struggle can be a joy to us if what we struggle for is worth the effort. "The struggle which is not joyous," Germaine Greer writes, "is the wrong struggle."

**FEBRUARY 22** There is no joy in purposely steeping ourselves in activities we resent. Or in taking on good works for the wrong reasons like social approval or public expectations. Thomas Merton says, "To allow oneself to be carried away by a multitude of conflicting concerns, to surrender to too many demands...is to succumb to violence."

**FEBRUARY 23** There is no need to live life like oxen tied to a revolving oil press. We must make our own small delights the joy that gives us the energy to go on making the circle. Even Thomas Aquinas says, "It is requisite for the relaxation of the mind that we make use, from time to time, of playful deeds and jokes." Jokes?!

**FEBRUARY 24** Boredom is the death of the soul. We must avoid that by creating our own interests. Jean Garrigue says, "If we get used to life, that is the crime."

**FEBRUARY 25** It is one thing to take life seriously; it is another thing entirely to invest it with gloom. Life is indeed what we make it. "Eat chocolate now," Jean Powell writes. "After you're dead, there isn't any."

**FEBRUARY 26** Every day should be filled with at least one hour of what we most want to do. Out of that time comes the lifeblood of the soul that dispels the gloom of all its darkest parts. "God," Teresa of Avila prays, "save us from gloomy saints."

**FEBRUARY 27** There is a task in life that is greater than any other task: We must find joy for ourselves and we must share it with others.

**FEBRUARY 28** Finding space for the blooming joy of the self is life's greatest accomplishment. Out of that joy and energy come all the other good we do and the joy we have to give to others. "If you are losing your leisure, look out! It may be you are losing your soul," wrote Logan Pearsall Smith.

MARCH

# Why Pray?

I grew up being told to pray...that there would be no rain for the picnic. Or, that my grandmother would not die from the cancer that was eating her up inside. Or that I would walk again. Or that the war would end. Or that Russia would be converted. Or that peace would come. And I prayed for all those things and was deeply disappointed when most of them did not happen. Prayer, they told me, was a conversation with God, but God, it seemed, seldom answered.

What was the matter with me if God did not answer those prayers? Better yet, what was the matter with God, who could have answered but did not?

It took years before I realized that actually the church had been teaching a far more profound theology of prayer than was ever talked about in the parish.

Prayer, I was taught, had four purposes: adoration of a God whose cosmic control, it seemed, demanded it; contrition for my sins—however hard I tried to be perfect, I failed; supplication for favors that did not always come; and thanksgiving for gifts I got but did not recognize.

There was nothing really wrong with such a schema, except that it was more a regimen, a series of exercises, than a dialogue with God. It seemed to me, thanks to that explanation, that prayer was all about the worship of a remote God who crouched in the dark somewhere, waiting to catch us in an act of defiance that would forever cast us out of heaven. It was about learning to fear the loving God who had made us from dust and never really expected us to be perfect. It was about begging to be spared the very essential elements of life, failure, growth, and death. It was about being thankful that things hadn't been even worse than they were.

The problem was that the basic teachings on prayer were definitely not about the development of a life lived in harmony, in relationship with the God of ongoing Life. They were not about learning to live a spiritual life that would actually insulate us from putting our hearts on the things of this world instead of on the God who gave us life and then helped us to live it well. Instead, it was about some kind of Santa Claus god who, if we were "good," whatever that meant under stress, would save us from our vile selves and crown our lives with worthless baubles that, in the end, would all simply disappear. All that effort for nothing, I sighed.

One thing for sure, this kind of prayer was not about finding the God who loves us uniquely and wholly and carries us through the dark places of spiritual growth and companions us through this life to the next.

But then, I began to read the mystics and discovered the other teachings of the church on the development of the spiritual life. Here the great spiritual masters of life taught that our ascent to God went through three stages: First, it required us, on the purgative level of the spiritual life, to let go of our immersion in the material dimensions of life so that we could come to the fullness of our being. At the second level of prayer, the illuminative, we learned that we would find ourselves absorbed in the contemplative awareness of God alive within us and around us. Then, finally, after years of growing beyond things and into God here and now, at the third stage of the spiritual life, we would finally come to the unitive level of our spiritual search and its melting of the human heart into the mind of God.

That kind of prayer life, I understood, was not an exercise; it was another entire way of life that saw God in the here and now and so, without doubt, someday, in the there and then. Whatever and wherever that next stage might be.

**MARCH 1** God is closer to us than we are to ourselves. It is for that reason that we reach out beyond the material, beyond the present. We are trying to find the point of our existence, the explanation of life. And that, of course, is contemplation.

**MARCH 2** Prayer is the natural response of people who know their place in the universe. It is not designed to be a psychological comfort zone though, surely, comfort it must. Most of all, it is an act of awareness of God and, sitting there in the midst of a praying community, awareness of the rest of the world, as well.

**MARCH 3** We do not pray in order to control God. We pray in order to become new within ourselves, to see differently, to see right.

**MARCH 4** Prayer is meant to bring us to see the world as God sees the world. It is meant to expand our vision, not trap us in a world that is only ourselves.

**MARCH 5** When our eyes are focused only on ourselves and the things we have made our own in life, we lose our perspective. We miss the real meaning of life.

**MARCH 6** God does not commonly come to us in prayer in words that match our own. God comes in insights and understandings and feelings that must be carefully culled.

**MARCH 7** Prayer is the step that takes us beyond the trappings of life to the essence of life. "Prayer," the mystic Julian of Norwich says, "oneth the soul to God." Without the lifeline that is prayer, we run the risk of never knowing what life was really meant to be about.

**MARCH 8** It is in this life that we take the first step into faith in the beyond. But after that first step, there is nothing else about life that can possibly daunt us because we have finally seen the God of the Universe at work.

**MARCH 9** Humility comes from prayer. It enables us to see strength, power, goodness, and justice in others because we have first seen it in God. As Madame Chiang Kai-shek said, "Prayer is more than meditation. When we pray, we go to a source of strength far greater than our own."

**MARCH 10** It is in prayer that we get to know God. Then, real prayer leads us to know ourselves, our deficiencies, our fears, and our needs. Then, we come to know that we are not our own god.

**MARCH 11** Prayer is not meant to be an "exercise," a proof of our sanctity. On the contrary, prayer is meant to be an emptying out of the very idea of our grandeur so that God can come in and bring us to the fullness of ourselves. As Teresa of Avila says, "Prayer is not just spending time with God. If it ends there, it is fruitless. Authentic prayer changes us, unmasks us, strips us, indicates where growth is needed."

**MARCH 12** In prayer, unmasked and empty, we come to know ourselves as well as we come to find God in our emptiness. But that knowing demands that we grow. As Teresa of Avila goes on, "Authentic prayer never leads to complacency, but needles us, makes us uneasy at times."

**MARCH 13** Every day that we settle down to pray we understand how really needy we are. Mahatma Gandhi wrote, "Prayer is the daily admission of one's weakness." Then, we have room in us for God, the one who fills up all our emptiness, all our weaknesses, and gives us the strength it takes to go on trusting that the one who made us will sustain us.

**MARCH 14** All we have to bring to prayer is our empty, listless, frightened, hopeful, faithful selves. Then, there is a huge window in the heart for the Spirit of God to enter.

**MARCH 15** We do not go to prayer, like children at Christmastime, to coax God to give us presents. As Søren Kierkegaard writes, "The function of prayer is not to influence God, but rather to change the nature of the one who prays."

**MARCH 16** We keep images of holy ones around us as we pray so that we may never doubt that the God who beckoned them is also beckoning us.

**MARCH 17** Jesus did not come looking for perfection. He came looking for faith. Peter who denied Jesus, Judas who betrayed him, Mary Magdalene who was disappointed in him—all of them are proof that we too must proceed with faith, not in ourselves, but in the God who made us and now waits for us to respond.

**MARCH 18** Prayer is not asking for things. It is reaching out to find the God who is looking for us. As St. Teresa of Calcutta put it, "Prayer is putting oneself in the hands of God,...listening to God's voice in the depth of our hearts."

**MARCH 19** There is no such thing as saying the "right prayer" that will take us to God. God is not a lotto ticket waiting for someone to say the right number. God is within us waiting for us to notice that.

**MARCH 20** There is only one prayer that is always answered, Anne Lamott writes, and that prayer is "help." God never abandons us, in other words, however much our life differs from our plan for it.

**MARCH 21** We must give our lives over to doing what we think must be done and then trust that the will of God is best for us, however long it takes.

**MARCH 22** There is no formula for the prayer of the heart. Prayer simply opens us to God. After that, everything in life becomes the presence of God to us.

**MARCH 23** "When we pray to God," St. Francis said, "we must be seeking nothing—nothing." Nothing but the desire to will what God wills and then to accept what comes.

**MARCH 24**  Prayer is not about ritual. Prayer is about the honest awareness that we have so much of ourselves to give back to God yet.

**MARCH 25**  Prayer is really an offering of the self to God given for the sake of the world. Then, as Henri Nouwen wrote, "When we pray, we are standing with our hands open to the world."

**MARCH 26**  There are verbal prayers and silent prayers and prayerless prayers. What makes them all true is the degree of faith we give to each as we wait within us for God to answer.

**MARCH 27**  There is a kind of false prayer. As Daniel Berrigan put it, "Prayer consists for the most part in insisting that God do for us what we are unwilling to do for one another. Resolve: Let's do for one another what we would have God do for us."

**MARCH 28**  Prayer can be talked about but only real prayer can be experienced. Thomas Merton wrote: "Prayer does not blind us to the world, but it transforms our vision of the world and makes us see it, all people, and all the history of humanity, in the light of God."

**MARCH 29** The desire to learn how to pray becomes too often in this world of formulas and computer languages a quest for just one more "how to" program in spirituality. As Merton says again, "Monastic prayer, especially meditation and contemplative prayer, is not so much a way to find God as a way of resting in the One whom we have found, who loves us, who is near to us, who comes to us."

**MARCH 30** Prayer, the old manuals say, "is the lifting of the mind and heart to God." And that's it. Try it once an hour and watch your life change faster than any amount of word repetition can possibly achieve.

**MARCH 31** Pray without ceasing, the Scripture says? Don't worry about it. As Peace Pilgrim writes, "Praying without ceasing is not ritualized, nor are there even words. It is a constant state of awareness of oneness with God."

# The Absence of Divine Presence

One of my favorite stories never grows old. I tell it to myself over and over again: Tommy, the three-year-old, seemed agitated. He insisted on being alone with the infant brother who had now come into the family. He was so intent on it that the parents began to question his behavior. Was it love or was it jealousy? Would he hurt the baby if he were left alone with him? So they set up a baby monitor by the crib and left the room to watch for signs of distress.

Sure enough, as soon as he was alone with the baby, Tommy went straight to the crib, shook the baby awake and said, "Eddie, I'm your big brother Tommy. I want you to tell me what God looks like. You know because you just came from there but I'm three now and I'm beginning to forget."

The awareness of Divine Presence is almost a thing of the past.

Nevertheless, we have a language for it that is clear, concise, and seldom used as more than a series of clichés rather than with real intent. For instance, we say, "God bless you," when we sneeze. At Christmastime we sing, "Emmanuel, God with us," at least in church. Sometimes we even say "God love you" instead of "Thank you." Every once in a while, in our concern for others, it slips out: "God help them," we say under our breath.

In extremis we plead, "God, be with me"—often more out of pain than as a sign of deep-down conscious awareness that all other salvation has already been abolished in our lives.

Hardly ever now, but still a bit, we hear someone—usually someone older than we—venture into this entirely other way of looking at life. Even now. Even in the midst of rampant secularism. Even here, in this country where cursing is common but blessings are rare.

Too often, in fact, we say "God bless you" ourselves and feel a little embarrassed for having allowed it to slip out. I do it, I know, when I thank the young man who carries the large boxes downstairs for me. Or I hear myself say it as the last word I toss back at the cab driver. Or as my final personal word to the one who's leaving the office after a deep and private conversation. Or I do it to the child whose blond curls I've just tousled.

And, of course, the prioress of the monastery says it over the community after every prayer period of the day.

But most of us have learned not to say those words much anymore. I don't remember how that happened. As far as I know, no one made it a proscription but, little by little, it has become improper to commend anyone to God outside of formal prayer.

Yet, this string of leftover phrases from another age remains as a kind of silent proof that the consciousness of God is still wired into our hearts, embedded in our souls, struggling for attention in our very rational brains.

And that, I think, is a hopeful sign. Maybe the Divine Presence can arise again to make a highly technological society conscious of the fact that in the end it will not be technology that saves us.

Maybe those very words will remind me of the holiness of spirit in the person whose presence is annoying me right now.

Maybe calling it regularly to mind will release again the spiritual sensitivities that a largely material world has managed to drown out.

Perhaps we will, with Tommy, remember again Who really brought us here and depends on us to go on leavening the world around us with Spirit.

And so, until then...God bless you.

**APRIL 1**  Once we lose the sense of the real presence of God in our lives, our lives dry up and become purposeless. But it is not that God has forgotten us. The fact is that we have forgotten God.

**APRIL 2**  The terrible loneliness sets in when we have detached ourselves from the Divine Presence. This is exactly the time when I must consciously place myself in the arms of God, who brought me into life and who now upholds me there.

**APRIL 3** The presence of God in our lives never really leaves us. It simply lies dormant within us because we ourselves never advert to it.

**APRIL 4** When I remove myself from the consciousness of the presence of God, I doom myself to no one but myself in the exercise of life.

**APRIL 5** The strength of God's grace is diminished when I no longer attend to the impulses of the Spirit. I can no longer feel the tug of the Spirit within me because I long ago stopped listening to it. "What is sacred about all of our lives," Frederick Buechner writes, "is that God speaks to us through what happens to us."

**APRIL 6** What happens to us in life is an invitation to explore its spiritual meaning for us. In that lies the gentle voice of God. Too often I have numbed myself to the God within by reacting to life rather than meditating on life.

**APRIL 7** We know that God, to be God, must be everywhere. Then why would we think that does not mean in me, for me. "God, Who is everywhere," Thomas Merton writes, "never leaves us."

**APRIL 8** The God who never leaves us is always leading us into another level of Divine Presence.

**APRIL 9** God is not a ventriloquist. God's call is not an answer to a math problem or to a personal relationship gone bad. God's call comes as a breath of insight. A surge of new strength. The awareness that we are strong, even in our weakness, because we know that God is with us now more than ever.

**APRIL 10** The power of the Divine Presence lies in the fact that there is no barrier to it. On the contrary, everything in life is our hidden access to the God who promises us life and sustains us in its doing.

**APRIL 11** Life is made up of the presence of God if we would only acknowledge it—and reply. As Merton says, "If we do not know God well, we do not realize that God may be more present to us when absent than when present."

**APRIL 12**  God is palpable. The problem is that we have learned to think of God as something else. Edna St. Vincent Millay writes, "God, I can push the grass apart and lay my finger on Thy heart."

**APRIL 13**  We seek God the Warrior when we should be looking for God the Mystery and the answer to everything. Nikos Kazantzakis writes, "God changes appearances every second. Blessed is the one who can recognize God in all disguises."

**APRIL 14**  The pangs of happiness, the sharpness of pain. Both of them are manifestations of God. Both of them we miss far too often to really understand life.

**APRIL 15**  It is the little things of life, the subatomic dimensions of life—its quarks and neutrinos—in which God waits for us to be surprised. To be renewed. "One moment, God is a glass of fresh water," Kazantzakis says, "the next, your son bouncing on your knees...or perhaps merely a morning walk." It is bothering to stop long enough to see it, to remark on it, that makes life spiritual.

**APRIL 16** There is certainly the presence of God on earth. It happens in moments of love. As Albert Schweitzer said, "Only through love can we obtain communion with God."

**APRIL 17** We are here on earth to come to know God—so that we can melt into the beauty of the universe that is prepared for us. "If the soul could have known God without the world," Meister Eckhart wrote, "the world would never have been created."

**APRIL 18** Over time we become aware that we do not grow ourselves. Only life grows us, one value, one truth, one strength at a time. In that certainty lies the understanding that God is both the essence of the life of the soul and its end.

**APRIL 19** Rituals and images are not our access to God. They are at most steps along the way designed to bring us to know God both with and without images and rituals.

**APRIL 20** Everything in life is a glimpse into the mind and heart of God. "There are only two ways to live your life," Albert Einstein said. "One is as though nothing is a miracle. The other is as though everything is a miracle." Choose.

**APRIL 21** In every human being there is great and gnawing emptiness. It is that gulf that life is meant to fill with God.

**APRIL 22** To find the God we are looking for, we must realize first that God is within us. Second, we must understand that we will never find God, even there, unless we discover what it is that is crowding God out. "The inspiration you seek is already within you," the poet Rumi writes. "Be silent and listen."

**APRIL 23** We insist that it is God we seek in life, God who is missing from our life, God who has abandoned us and our small lives. But down deep we know that it is God who is waiting for us, not we who are waiting for God. "God is in your heart," Guru Arjan teaches, "yet you search for God in the wilderness."

**APRIL 24** Ask yourself what you are aiming for in life and you will know two things: where God is and where you are not.

**APRIL 25** The miracle of the spiritual life lies in the length of time we ignore it—only to discover that it has been there all the time waiting for our attention. But not to worry: Hippocrates wrote, "The human soul develops up to the time of death." Point: Get on with it.

**APRIL 26** The boulders of life, the mountains of obstacles with which even a normal life taxes us, are all there to help us grow into God, one experience at a time. To allow those things to consume us is a mistake. As Friedrich Nietzsche wrote, "The 'kingdom of Heaven' is a condition of the heart—not something that comes 'upon the earth' or 'after death.'"

**APRIL 27** Heaven and union with God both depend on how much awareness of the spiritual life I am prepared to give up, give away, or ignore. Instead of waiting for the presence of God to come in some mysterious way and time,

I should be aware that God is already in the here and now. If I will only recognize it.

**APRIL 28** Just be yourself. Keep one part of your mind in tune with the mind of God for the world and the other part of your heart concerned for the heart of others, and no books or rituals, images or pious practices will be needed.

**APRIL 29** The Talmud teaches, "Every blade of grass has its angel that bends over it and whispers, 'Grow, grow.'" As do we. Remember that God wishes you "well and not woe" and everything that happens to you in life will become another sliver of your union with God. And, as Ramana Maharshi writes, "As you are, so is the world."

**APRIL 30** Prayerfulness is the capacity to walk in touch with God through everything in life. It is the internal awareness that God is with me. As Thomas Moore wrote, "We would be able to live in this world more peaceably if our spirituality were to come from looking not just into infinity but very closely at the world around us and appreciating its depth and divinity."

## The Virtue of Self-Acceptance

The ninth degree of humility in the Rule of Benedict invites us "to speak gently." Our consciousness of this dimension of life has never been less than it is now. In fact, we are losing it and so weakening the very fabric of our society, our trust in one another, our care for the community.

Here's why I'm so sure:

It's hard to watch the news, to read the papers, to listen to congressional hearings these days.

Whatever once existed of American civility, decorum, decency, and the serious and respectful deliberation of national issues is apparently over. Honesty has become a magic act; one day it's this; another day it's that. Truth is now a series of "tweets"—little bits of nothing but snippets of insults and accusations, attacks and denials.

Now so-called "representatives"—of what, I'm

no longer sure—and long-standing senators—the anointed guards of wisdom and the keepers of national values and character—deteriorate into middle school playground teams slinging mud as they go.

The airwaves bristle with insult and denial.

Worst of all, at the head of the pack rides the former president himself, the biggest mudslinger of them all, slaying imaginary dragons and peppering his critics with nicknames and labels as he goes.

As he says, "Sad...sad."

So, pity them, each and every one. Such grandiose falls from grace are rare. As the former president likes to point out, though not in this context, this fall is "the greatest of them all."

The only problem is that politics like this are eroding the quality of the country in the process. Which is also all right, apparently, as long as the stock market keeps going up while the operational values of the country keep going down.

Which means what for the rest of the country? It means, there is no one left to save us from ourselves but us. If the country, our children, our neighborhoods, and our churches are to salvage anything of the spirit and character of this country as the world has known it, we must all refuse to join the fray.

On the ground, in our cities and homes, decency must remain a value, kindness common, and compassion our lived experience as walls against moral corruption, mean politics, and ruthless selfishness.

Humility, the antidote to narcissism that the Rule of Benedict modeled for the world in the sixth century, brought order and compassion to a Europe in turmoil for over a thousand years.

Now humility can do it again just as it did then: by starting at the bottom, with us—with you and me—and working up.

**MAY 1** Humility is the glue that binds the human race together, in one family, in common care. When we know ourselves, we see our own needs in the eyes of the rest of the world and respond accordingly.

**MAY 2** Humility never forces anything on anyone. Instead, it listens—and learns.

**MAY 3** To be humble is not to be weak. It only means that we are strong enough to listen to someone else and learn.

**MAY 4** Humility takes me out of concentration on myself alone. It enables me to make honest contact with someone else where true relationship begins.

**MAY 5** Pride dries up the soul that lives on itself alone. It takes the juice out of life.

**MAY 6** It's our relationship with others that brings happiness and joy. But that only comes from being able to love someone beside ourselves.

**MAY 7** To defer to the ideas of another above our own only makes us stronger, as well. Now we not only know what we know, but we know what they know too.

**MAY 8** Humility saves me the foolishness of thinking of myself as my own god. "True humility is not thinking less of yourself," Rick Warren says. "It is thinking of yourself less."

**MAY 9** To be humble means that I will never need to lie—either to myself about me or to anyone else about me. I will accept what is in me and do my best to bring it to fullness in life.

**MAY 10** It's not difficult to be humble. What's difficult is to have to pretend to others that I am more than what I really am.

**MAY 11** Humility stops us from making more of ourselves than we are. Better yet, it stops us from thinking of ourselves as less than we really are and so failing to do what we can for the rest of the world around us.

**MAY 12** For me to take no responsibility for the rest of life is the highest arrogance. It means that I want others to carry me through the hard patches of life with no promise whatsoever to do my part for them, as well. "Humility,"

Madeleine L'Engle writes, "is throwing oneself away in complete concentration on something or someone else."

**MAY 13** Humility—the honest appraisal of who I am and who I am not—saves us from taking on more than we can do. It also requires us to increase what we should be doing because others need it and we have the gifts for it.

**MAY 14** When we sincerely attend to others, to their thoughts and needs, we give the world the gift of attention. It is a rare commodity in a world built around the amplification of the self—electronically, globally, and anonymously.

**MAY 15** Humility is the bedrock of kindness. When we truly admit to ourselves who and what we are, we know what others are going through. Then, reaching out to the other becomes real again.

**MAY 16** To know myself is the best way to understand why being kind, being gentle is the ultimate human gift. We all need so much support from one another, but the best of it comes from someone who understands how much kindness is really needed at a time like this because self-knowledge has made them aware of what another is suffering.

**MAY 17**  We think more than we love. That's what's wrong with the family, the neighborhood, the city. When we speak gently, on all those levels, life gets better every day. St. Teresa of Avila is clear: "Be gentle to all and stern with yourself."

**MAY 18**  Our world runs on pride. Who's best, first, greatest, richest, tallest, smartest? Whatever. As a result, the perfidy of ranking blinds us to the values and gifts of everyone from second place on down. We miss the very heart of life.

**MAY 19**  Once we're truthful about ourselves, no one can ever again sully our reputation. We simply are what we are. As Thomas Merton says, "Pride makes us artificial and humility makes us real."

**MAY 20** There is no one who does not need the gentle presence of a humble person. Because humility is truth, we can bear the truths of our own lives and understand the truth of theirs. Henry Wadsworth Longfellow wrote, "If we could read the secret history of our enemies, we should find in each one's life sorrow and suffering enough to disarm all hostility."

**MAY 21** We cannot heal the whole wide world. But we can heal the need for love and understanding of the person who stands in front of us. By that very act the world begins to change. "Since you cannot do good to all," St. Augustine says, "you are to pay special attention to those who, by the accidents of time, or place, or circumstances, are brought into closer connection with you."

**MAY 22** To be ourselves at all times—no airs, no rage, no demands—and to allow others to be the same is to give everyone we meet a safe place to be. In that moment of genuine embrace is the seed of more. "A single act of kindness may have a long trajectory," Rachel Naomi Remen writes, "and touch those we will never meet or see...and so each of us may have left far more behind us than we may ever know."

**MAY 23**  The first demand of the mature spiritual life is to come to know the self. Then, following that kind of self-knowledge, St. Catherine of Siena says, "flows the stream of humility which never takes offense at anything but bears every insult...from whatever direction they may come."

**MAY 24**  There's no need to brag your way through life. As Judith Martin says, "It is far more impressive when others discover your good qualities without your help."

**MAY 25**  What's at least as bad as narcissistic pride is false humility. When we pretend to be one thing—sweet, kind, honest, generous, forgiving—while inside we are clearly the opposite, we make a mockery of the truth. "Nothing is more deceitful than the appearance of humility," Jane Austen writes.

**MAY 26** Humility is the virtue of self-acceptance. We acknowledge our humanity, our likeness to all the rest of the world, and all that implies about what we lack.

**MAY 27** It's when we truly accept what we ourselves lack that, ironically, we begin to realize, as Herman Melville says, "We cannot live only for ourselves. A thousand fibers connect us with our fellow human beings."

**MAY 28** Want to know how much humility you yourself have been able to develop? Take the M. Scott Peck test: "You cannot truly listen to anyone and do anything else at the same time." Ever done that? Even once?

**MAY 29** Whenever we think we're powerful enough to stand alone, we learn a little more about our weakness. And that is exactly what makes us more human in the end.

**MAY 30** Humility ties us to humankind, yes, but it also elevates us to the arms of God. John Flavel says it this way: "They that know God will be humble, and they that know themselves cannot be proud."

**MAY 31** The temptations to pride, to domination, to superiority are sold in every media ad on the planet: Buy this, own this, get this and be bigger, better, richer than everybody else. Rise above the crowd. Excel. And then the fear sets in. As John Ortberg says: "We'd like to be humble...but what if no one notices?"

## JUNE

# When Religion Becomes a Symbol Rather Than a Sign

Here's the problem: How can we possibly talk about hospitality this month and do it with any integrity at all? How can we dare to talk about things like being nice to strangers, about welcoming new people into our neighborhoods—when we have built walls to keep people out of those neighborhoods and our country? Worse, we have labeled refugees as rapists and murderers as they come down dirt roads carrying everything they own strapped to their backs, including their infant children.

So, what is the problem?

If we could only admit it, most of religion is symbolic. It's goodwilled, of course, but so often confusing. Fact and fiction can easily become the same thing when symbols are used to substitute for the real thing. For instance, we fast during Lent to identify with the sacrifice of Jesus but never know anything less than three meals a day. We give up coffee or desserts but abstain from nothing difficult enough to actually curb the damaging impulses that underlie our flares of anger or our party-time binges. We may even say the Stations of the Cross as if we were walking the road to Calvary with Jesus but only at a nice safe distance from suffering of any kind. We kneel to announce our humility while we lord over most of the people of the earth in power and security and think nothing of it.

We like religion that's antiseptic and quiet. None of this loud, public Jesus stuff for us. No insistence. No condemnations of systemic sin. No doubt about it: Symbolism is its own kind of subterfuge.

Our symbolism these days for hospitality is especially alluring. We have no problem with immigrants, we say. We simply want legal ones. But we do nothing in the meantime to devise a new kind of legal system that handles both the trauma of devastation and the destitution that comes from it. We ignore their needs and our own value system by refusing to create a system that satisfies the sense of order that good hospitality demands.

We do nothing to develop new immigration procedures rather than simply send people away who have come to where they think that hope, abundant and generous, must surely await them.

These are people who have literally risked their lives to come to our gate and beg for life-giving asylum.

In the end they are asking for nothing but a chance.

And in the end there is a real part of us that

haunts us in the background, if what we want is more real religion and less symbolism.

The line that haunts us reads: "And the angel appeared in a dream and said to Joseph, 'Get up, take the child and his mother with you and escape into Egypt and stay there until I tell you'" (Mt 2:13).

So what representatives or senators have you called to protest the sinfulness of our refugee system now, here, today—while the government pours billions into a wall that will keep people out rather than spend a pittance on hot soup and placement plans as we did for the Vietnamese over forty years ago?

Suddenly, that headline Scripture is not symbolic anymore. It's real again. It is, in fact, the very cornerstone of our religion. But this time, unfortunately, its reality depends on us.

JUNE 1 Hospitality is a public virtue that is grounded in an individual's capacity for personal love. We cannot hope to be able to love people we can't see until we are willing and able to reach out in love to the people we see. The ones who move in next door to us. As Gandhi says, "If you do not find God in the next person you meet, it is a waste of time looking further."

**JUNE 2**  Hospitality is about more than nice smiles and warm handshakes. It is about the development of an open heart.

**JUNE 3**  It's not hospitality to like the people who like us, to support people who are just like us. Hospitality takes into our plans the concerns of those who are least like us. Those without food and furniture, perhaps.

**JUNE 4**  Hospitality has become big business in the United States. Which means, of course, that those who need it can't get it. What becomes of virtue then?

**JUNE 5**  Here's an idea: What if every religious congregation that used to build schools each put up a short-term hostel for immigrants? Then, maybe people who are homeless could be sure that their children had food and a roof until they could find the job that would enable them to find some kind of decent lodgings for themselves.

**JUNE 6** The first thing that has to open before the immigrant question can be resolved are the closed minds of those who have forgotten, as the Scriptures remind us, that we too were sojourners once (Ex 22:21).

**JUNE 7** Hospitality must be grounded in need, not in politics. As Eleanor Roosevelt put it, "True hospitality consists of giving the best of yourself to your guests."

**JUNE 8** When we stop seeking services for immigrants, we have stopped searching for God. Without that commitment, we only look as if we're searching for God. "To find God," Rabindranath Tagore writes, "you must welcome everything."

**JUNE 9** Nothing will bring world peace faster than the opening of our lives to cultures and religions unlike ours. "There is nothing that we can do but love," Dorothy Day said, "and, dear God, please enlarge our hearts to love each other, to love our neighbor, to love our enemy as well as our friend."

**JUNE 10**  Culture and religion are not barriers to peace. They are the best signs we have that we are all really alike in the one place it counts: in the heart.

**JUNE 11**  When a government stokes fear of one people in another, that government is committed to nothing but its own power. It is not committed to the good of the human race. Then government itself is to be feared.

**JUNE 12**  When the nations of the world were all working together for a common good, every nation on earth began to develop. Now, imperial governments are beginning to rise again in our midst that want to draw all the money, all the power, all the force, all the institutions, and all the ideas everywhere. Warning: If you have a vote, take it very, very seriously or it could be your undoing.

**JUNE 13** Love is not cuddly. Love is very serious stuff, especially on the national level. "When we choose to love, we choose to move against fear, against alienation and separation. The choice to love is a choice to connect, to find ourselves in the other," bell hooks states.

**JUNE 14** Hospitality is not a display of generosity toward others. It is the awareness that without our own connection to the wider world there is very little reason for us to be alive at all. After all, why have we been given a heart and a mind if not for the obligation to use both for others. William Blake reminds us, "Everything that lives, lives not alone, nor for itself."

**JUNE 15** Hospitality has been cheapened in modern society, reduced to things called "hospitality tents"—sponsored giveaways at events where only the invited, those who already have in abundance, get more and this time get it for nothing. The very words fool us into thinking that free sandwiches for people who don't need to get anything for nothing are the extent of it.

**JUNE 16** We, each and together, are the very nature of the world we fear. Which means that we can change that environment anytime we decide to do so. As Helen Keller said, "Until the great mass of the people shall be filled with the sense of responsibility for each other's welfare, social justice can never be attained."

**JUNE 17** Community makes it possible for us to do great things together, things we could never do alone. On the other hand, community also denies us a sense of personal responsibility for anything. It's then that real hospitality, real outreach, and understanding end. That's when we say we want it done, as long as someone else does it first. Dietrich Bonhoeffer says of it, "Many people seek fellowship because they are afraid to be alone. Let the one who cannot be alone beware of community."

**JUNE 18** Hospitality is the sacrament of the self. In it we give ourselves away to those who need to rest their burdens for a while. In turn, they give us another view of the world that will stretch and test and fill us with thoughts enough to grow on.

**JUNE 19** Particular groups have great needs but everybody needs support of one kind or another. It's not their need that must be measured to qualify us as hospitable. It's our willingness to give help on any and every level that is the real measure of hospitality. Or as G.K. Chesterton put it: "We make our friends; we make our enemies; but God makes our next door neighbor."

**JUNE 20** Hospitality is not what we do for someone else. Hospitality is about opening ourselves to the universe and its needs so that our own vision may expand. "Our task," Albert Einstein writes, "must be to free ourselves by widening our circle of compassion to embrace all living creatures and the whole of nature and its beauty."

**JUNE 21** There are three kinds of hospitality: hospitality of the body, hospitality of the mind, and hospitality of the heart. Each of them is important. All of them are the stuff of holiness.

**JUNE 22** Hospitality of the body requires us to serve the physical needs of people in ways that make their own lives happy as well as safe. "What do we live for, if not to make life less difficult for each other?" George Eliot asks us.

**JUNE 23** Hospitality of the mind requires that we go out of the way to understand the unknown other. To really meet a person we must ask at least one important question, find out at least one thing that has meaning to them, and exchange at least one genuine feeling. "We must," Marianne Williamson cautions, "make a space in our heart, in our mind and in our life itself if we are to make a genuine human connection."

**JUNE 24** Hospitality of the heart listens for feeling and probes both the cause of it and the pain of it. "Open your heart—open it wide,"

Mary Engelbreit writes; "someone is standing outside."

**JUNE 25** There is only one way to meet the unknown other and that is with a smile and a question that speaks of personal interest. An interest genuine enough to make the person welcome in your life.

**JUNE 26** "The most radical thing you can do is introduce people to each other," Glenn Hilke says. Once that has been done well and lovingly, the world is two people closer to caring for one another.

**JUNE 27** Public service is meant to be for the good of the served. But days of the demagogues are on the horizon, promising people everything they want so that the leader can get everything she/he wants. George Bernard Shaw lived by another model. He wrote, "I am of the opinion that my life belongs to the whole community and as long as I live, it is my privilege to do for it whatever I can."

**JUNE 28**  It's not meeting others that is important. It is encountering them—probing their ideas, their hopes, the joy that binds us to one another. As the philosopher Camus writes, "When you have once seen the glow of happiness on the face of a beloved person, you know that we can have no vocation but to awaken that light on the faces surrounding us."

**JUNE 29**  Remember that everyone you meet is dying. As are you. We do not have time enough for squabbling over the eminently forgettable. Nor does the planet have time to wait for us to develop vision enough to maintain us all.

**JUNE 30**  Reach out wherever you are to the people you know least as well as to the people you know best. As Paul Rogat Loeb says, "We become human only in the company of other human beings."

# Coming Home to Myself

The stories never end. One after another tell the same tale, describe the same situations, over and over again. They say, "I started out in one thing but I wound up in another."

It all starts in school. I think I like math until I get a stunning history teacher. I started out in pharmacy and wound up in music. My first job was teaching algebra and I wound up coaching the basketball team. I began in business and then discovered literature and drama.

Or as the Portuguese say, "God writes straight with crooked lines."

The real exercise of life is moving a step at a time till I come to the place that feels like home. Like I belong here. Like it's not about learning something; it's just about doing it.

The notion of vocation is bigger than any college curriculum, deeper than any job, happier than any single event.

Vocation is about finding out who I really am—forget the pay scales, never mind having to take extra credit, or stop worrying about the time it will take away from other things for me to join Habitat for Humanity. It's about doing what needs to be done because I love doing it and the world needs it.

Vocation is a call from God that lives inside of me. It's something I find out that I like doing and do well enough to keep at it. A vocation is a feeling, a realization, a "call" from within me that never really goes away no matter what else I try to do instead of it. It transcends all the money another kind of life might promise. It ignores the amount of time it will take to be part of it. It is sacred space in the soul which, when I'm doing it, brings me to the center of my soul. It brings me home to myself.

One person I have in mind worked in his father's pizza place all his young days, played violin in a small band in high school, practiced incessantly, it seemed, but did the sensible thing and settled into the restaurant routine. Then without much notice or thought he, along with his brother, inherited it. But the brother had never really worked there, not like he did. So it was clear, wasn't it? He would go on with the family business.

Until, one summer, years later, the "Closed" sign showed up on the glass of the large front door. Impossible. This place was a city institution.

I never really knew what had happened to him. Until one night, as I left the theater, a man with a beard stepped out of the orchestra pit to stop me. The violinist from the pizza shop.

Vocation haunts us, never really lets us go, makes us the fullness of ourselves. Some day. Some way.

**JULY 1** There is in everyone a call to something bigger than themselves. That is a vocation.

**JULY 2** When we discover the gifts in ourselves that are meant to be used for the good of others, we have moved out of adolescence into spiritual adulthood.

**JULY 3** We are not born for our own satisfaction. We are born to bring satisfaction to others. W.H. Auden writes, "You owe it to all of us to get on with what you're good at."

**JULY 4** The impulse to help others is a sign of moral development.

**JULY 5** Musicians want to play good music for others; scientists labor all their lives to cure people of disastrous diseases; engineers work to make the cities work better. Those are all demonstrations of the gifts of God to us that live in others.

**JULY 6** Narcissism is the dark side of a personality. It whispers in the human ear, "My life is about me alone." Then the narcissists wait for everyone else to come and fill their needs, their desires, the adoration they seek. And so, in the end, they are always disappointed.

**JULY 7** The persons who shower gifts on others as they go are always rewarded by the joy of doing something that makes someone else's life brighter, better, more full of love. Dorothy Day wrote, "You will know your vocation by the joy that it brings you."

**JULY 8** The path you love best in life is the path you are meant to cultivate for the sake of the rest of your world.

**JULY 9** To find my vocation in life, I have to understand what I most enjoy doing—working alone or working with others, for instance. That will be my first clue about the kind of work situation I need to be in to be happy.

**JULY 10** Then, the second clue is to recognize the kind of things I do best—work with numbers, work with words, organize things, use art, music, and creativity to make things, or help others navigate life instead. That will be a clue to where to begin to put my efforts. "Our deepest calling is to grow into our own authentic self-hood, whether or not it conforms to some image of who we ought to be," Parker Palmer teaches.

**JULY 11**  If you can't find work that involves what you like to do to be happy, do it after your paying job. Or as Palmer also says, "Before I can tell my life what I want to do with it, I must listen to my life telling me who I am."

**JULY 12**  The greatest mistake of life is to become what someone else thinks I should become rather than what I want to become. Even if I'd make more money doing something else.

**JULY 13**  Life is not about money, no matter how much of it you have, get, inherit, or earn. Life is about doing what makes us happy to be alive.

**JULY 14**  How do I know what to do with my life? Easy. As Aristotle wrote centuries ago, "Where your talents and the needs of the world cross, there lies your vocation."

**JULY 15**  There is something I like to do and something I do unusually well that the rest of the world needs, wants, or is waiting for because they cannot do it for themselves. That's my "call" in life. Listen to it: for your sake as well as everybody else's. Gustaf Wingren writes, "God doesn't need our good works, but our neighbor does."

**JULY 16**  The modern world glamorizes high octane jobs, big money, public applause, but what makes the world go 'round best are people who give their gifts and talents to doing good for the people around them. The raises and promotions that come with working at what I like best pay better than the wrong best-paid job ever can.

**JULY 17**  Life is all about doing what we were made to do that gives the greatest happiness. St. Catherine of Siena taught, "Be who God meant you to be and you will set the world on fire."

**JULY 18**  If you have been given more than one talent and love them all, do what does the greatest good, gives the greatest joy to others.

**JULY 19**  No job is perfect if by "perfect" you mean easy, exciting, effortless, and energizing all the time. Everything worth doing is tedious, demanding, and sometimes even dull. Then, before you quit it, remember this: "The test of a vocation is the love of the drudgery it involves," Logan Pearsall Smith says. And sometimes its "drudgery" is more restful than its greatest achievements.

**JULY 20**  When life is dry and dreary, remember Eleanor Roosevelt's warning: "It is not more vacation we need—it is more vocation." Life without a sense of purpose is a barren life indeed.

**JULY 21**  Sometimes the vocation we have isn't the work we do. It's what we do after work. Like the violinist in the local symphony who runs the family pizza parlor during the day. Thomas Merton says of it, "Discovering vocation does not mean scrambling toward some prize just beyond my reach but accepting the treasure of true self I already possess."

**JULY 22**  The modern world has lost sight of what it means to have a "vocation" and turned everything into a "job" instead. How sad it is to reduce what I do to simply being paid to do it.

**JULY 23** Whatever you really wanted to do in life but could never manage, do it now. Get as close to it as you can get. As Honoré de Balzac wrote, "Vocations which we wanted to pursue, but didn't, bleed, like colors, on the whole of our existence."

**JULY 24** It is one thing to be employed. It is another thing entirely to be happy. Being happy requires that we do more than we have to because we really want to do what should be done. "True happiness," Helen Keller said, "is not attained through self-gratification but through fidelity to a worthy purpose."

**JULY 25** To go to sleep every night knowing that I have done something that day that will make the lives of other people better is the sign of the fully successful life.

**JULY 26** Jobs sustain us; vocations complete us. "The mystery of human existence," Fyodor

Dostoyevsky wrote, "lies not in just staying alive but in finding something to live for."

**JULY 27**   What creation has planted in us is what we have been given to give for the sake of others.

**JULY 28**   It's easy to assume that someone else can do what needs to be done and so ourselves ignore it. But the truth is that only we can do it our way—and that is the essential gift of it. Viktor Frankl says: "Everyone has their own specific vocation or mission in life: everyone must carry out a concrete assignment that demands fulfillment. Therein they cannot be replaced, nor can their life be repeated."

**JULY 29**   A real vocation is something that we cannot not do. Even if we never get to do it fully, it just keeps squeezing out of us into the atmosphere that needs it.

**JULY 30**   Leo Tolstoy puts it most directly, most simply of all. Tolstoy writes: "The vocation of every man and woman is to serve other people."

And I? What must I do? And how do I find it out? Oprah Winfrey says, "Each of us has a personal calling that's as unique as a fingerprint, and the best way to succeed is to discover what you love and find a way to offer it to others."

AUGUST

# Commit to Your Life

Two things are disappearing in modern society: the first is silence; the second is thought. Not necessarily because people don't believe in silence and thought anymore but because there is no time for them.

Chaos has become the order of our lives. We have a rather broad idea of tomorrow: keep the appointments, drive the kids to practice, get groceries, throw in the wash, do a few things around the house; go to bed early so we can start all over again the next day.

Or through the eyes of a younger generation,

get up, grab a donut, do the school run, spend an hour in the library looking for the arcane and irrelevant, grab a ride to the game, be late for supper, check social media again, do a bit of homework, meet the crowd at the coffee shop, get home late. And next day, start all over again.

No wonder we're tired at night. No wonder we don't bounce out of bed in the morning.

We are generations on the move, running in circles, trying to break out of the race. But only two things can get us off the merry-go-round: silence and thought. Except that there is no time for them.

They show up on no schedules. They are built into very few—if any—days. Why? Because there is simply no space for them—unless we make it. There are no natural moments for them anymore. No quiet hours before bedtime—just TV or being online to the end of the day.

No time to center before the day begins in the morning. Just more TV, internet, radio, the long commute or emails that must be answered quickly before the real work begins.

So what's the answer? You'll be disappointed. There are no tricks to it except your own commitment to yourself. It's up to you to pick the time and the place where you'll sit down and be quiet. Or sit down and read and think. Or just sit down and wait for silence to bring new life to your soul, new energy to your body, new peace to your mind, new awareness of what it is to be alive.

That's called meditation. Or the cultivation of "the beginner's mind." Or surrender to the self— just to see what comes up in me that I've been ignoring, repressing, overlooking for a long, long time.

There's too much noise in our lives? Well, maybe. But then, on the other hand, when was the last time you insisted on taking fifteen minutes, thirty minutes, an hour of silence? All for yourself?

Go ahead, I dare you.

In fact, write and tell me what happened after you did it for five days in a row...I predict great quiet of soul, great newness of mind.

**AUGUST 1**  Thinking does not happen if your life is like an electric blender. You have to take the time to let the mind seep through the maelstrom of living. Then, you will come to know you better.

**AUGUST 2**  To make time for yourself you will need to take that fifteen minutes from something else, of course. Question: Are you brave enough to do that so you can come out of it refreshed rather than frazzled for a change?

**AUGUST 3**  Fifteen minutes. "The beginning," Mary Wollstonecraft Shelley said, "is always today." Begin, why don't you, by taking charge of your life rather than simply letting life batter you unmercifully. Fifteen minutes. Only fifteen minutes a day could make all the difference.

**AUGUST 4**  The time we take in silence for ourselves will always repay us with calm.

**AUGUST 5**  When there's no time to think beyond the borders of our lives to better places for the soul to be, better things for the soul to do, we do nothing but simmer in the juices of confusion.

**AUGUST 6**  All the answers to all of our questions are within us. All you really need to do is to stop for a while, pose your questions to your soul, and then sit there and listen for the answer that you really already know.

**AUGUST 7**  When we find ourselves doing what we always do, there is no pool of time from which to draw new ideas. Then we're surprised when we feel so flat inside.

**AUGUST 8**  When there is no longer time enough to try a new recipe, plant a new kind of flower, visit a new museum, or read a new book, life has already died in you.

**AUGUST 9**  The question is a simple one: What kind of life have you always dreamed of living? When you know that, just buy it one little piece at a time.

**AUGUST 10**  What we fail to realize is how easy it is to grow stale as we go through life. Then, yesterday's schedule is what becomes the noose around our hearts. As Albert Einstein put it,

"An expert is a person who has few new ideas; a beginner is a person with many."

**AUGUST 11** The purpose of life is not to get it perfect and then put it into cement. The purpose of life is to live it newly every day so that every day is a new creation. The mystic Meister Eckhart taught, "Be willing to be a new beginner every single morning."

**AUGUST 12** We learn to strive more easily than we learn to live. Strivers want to shape a life for themselves that will never end. Learners want to master the essence of life so that its regular changes do not threaten its deepest truths.

**AUGUST 13** It is possible to float through every day—with its imposing tensions—rather than to race through it. We could try accepting the day as it happens and see if we have more energy or less every night.

**AUGUST 14** When we set out to control life, we fail. We refuse possibility. We resist the inevitable. We fight for the past rather than embrace the future. As Lao Tzu says, "New beginnings are often disguised as painful endings."

**AUGUST 15** Life is meant for trying, growing, seeking, failing, and trying again. Robin Sharma says of it, "Don't live the same year seventy-five times and call it a life."

**AUGUST 16** Don't wait for the perfect moment to find the rest of yourself inside yourself. There is no perfect moment for it. There is only your commitment to a better, saner, fuller life that will begin...right now. As C.S. Lewis says, "You can't go back and change the beginning, but you can start where you are and change the ending."

**AUGUST 17** In Western civilization children are trained to work toward a given goal and not to stop till they have achieved it. Which most of the time is making a lot of money. No one tells them what will happen when they finally get the money they worked for all those years. Which is a shame because the answer is "nothing." Point:

Only what you make happen along the way—like beauty, love, peace, simplicity, internal development—will you reap in the end.

**AUGUST 18** "If you want the whole thing, the gods will give it to you. But you must be ready for it," the folk wisdom teaches. There is absolutely nothing in life that is not destructive if done in excess. Freedom of spirit is the ability to see all the dimensions of life and to move from one to another without being enslaved by any of them.

**AUGUST 19** When you finish each day, be done with it. Then, add something you really wanted to do or read or talk about or plan. Then, the next day will be ripe with possibility.

**AUGUST 20** Gratitude is the key to life. Marcus Aurelius, the Roman emperor and philosopher, taught, "When you arise in the morning, think of what a precious privilege it is to be alive, to breathe, to think, to enjoy, to love."

**AUGUST 21** "Master," the disciple asked, "What can I do to free myself?" And the Holy One answered, "Who was it who put you in chains?" Answer: Only I myself can do that. Some of the finest writing ever done was done by those in prison.

**AUGUST 22** We are our own slave masters. It's time to free ourselves from whatever it is that holds us prisoner to yesterday's ambition for things rather than for joy.

**AUGUST 23** If we make every day new, every thought, insight, vision, and joy will also be new. Eleanor Roosevelt, a woman far more powerful and publicly effective outside of the White House than in it, wrote, "With the new day comes new strength and new thoughts."

**AUGUST 24** Fear is a barrier to life. We know what we want but fear that we will not be able to do it, to start it, to maintain it. Martin Luther King Jr. faced that one for the rest of us. He wrote, "Take the first step in faith. You don't have to see the whole staircase, just take the first step."

**AUGUST 25** Think of something doable that you would really like to do, have wanted to do for a long time, like visit the zoo, become a member of the philharmonic, learn to bowl, start a card club, get into a reading group. Then, immediately, do it. Then, watch life change. As Bill Johnson put it, "What you know will keep you from what you need to know."

**AUGUST 26** It is so easy to get caught in one set of old ideas: such as what we should have done in life rather than what we did do or can still do. Joseph Campbell writes: "We must be willing to get rid of the life we've planned, so as to have the life that is waiting for us. The old skin has to be shed before the new one can come."

**AUGUST 27** You know what you'd like to do: So, do it. Time is marching on....

**AUGUST 28** Boredom is one portal to depression. And depression is a factor, not of age, but of our own failure to keep living. "Beware of monotony," Edith Wharton wrote. "It's the mother of all the deadly sins."

**AUGUST 29** When we know what it means to have "enough" rather than simply to "have it all," we are on the road to a happier, freer life. As the Kenyan proverb says, "Those who have cattle have care."

**AUGUST 30** When we burden our lives with what we don't really need to do to the point that we have no time to do anything except take care of those things, we are like donkeys on an olive press. We go around in circles wearing ourselves out and wondering what it was that robbed us of life.

**AUGUST 31** But we know all this, don't we? Maybe what we've forgotten is even easier. As in J.P. Morgan's insight that "The first step towards getting somewhere is to decide you're not going to stay where you are."

# The Virtue of Protest

History is made by people who, faced with unacceptable human situations, become part of the chorus of voices who refused to assent to it.

It is the Fourth of July as I write this. It is a day to celebrate consciousness and conscience, to remember that not only was our country born in protest, but it has been shaped by protest:

African Americans banded together to overthrow white segregation laws.

American Indians, the real natives of the United States, struggled together to maintain both their identity and their continuing recognition as sovereign entities.

Women joined forces to achieve legal rights and full citizenship in a culture that defined them as male property and adult children in a male world.

The physically handicapped, the elderly, laborers, and immigrants, all outliers in the "home of the free and the brave," came together to claim their autonomy, the fullness of their humanity, and their equal rights in a society originally constitutionally designed to give voting rights only to "landed gentry," to white men who owned land.

Gays, and eventually the LGBTQ community, stood together to resist discrimination. They demanded legal recognition of their relationships and legal protection under the law.

History is clear: the right to, the need for, and the character of dissent and protest are what really made this country great. Without protest, both justice and real societal, personal development is impossible.

Nor were churches themselves free from the kind of internal and political protest that required them to compare their moral behaviors to the gospel ideals they professed. For centuries, the notion of state religions and ecclesiastical privilege waxed and waned.

In Europe, Catherine of Siena went all the way to France to protest the "Avignon Papacy" that threatened to politicize the church and undermine the symbolic power and neutrality of its Roman roots.

Martin Luther in the sixteenth century called the church to reforms it acceded to only four hundred years later in the Second Vatican Council, but which now have become part and parcel of what it means to be Catholic.

In eighteenth-century United States, we enshrined in law, after a mighty struggle with a mighty empire in disagreement with us, that no one church could speak for the government and the government could not favor any single church.

And now, still, in the twenty-first century, hundreds of thousands of people protest war, march for peace, and plead for equality and justice for whole segments of people.

Even as you read this, thousands more are standing between the US government and the immigrant children we are putting in cages, the poor parents we leave to die on the roads in search of jobs and food and medical care, the raiding and deportation of families without a country.

These truth-tellers are not committing "treason." They are protesting the loss of what it means to have an American conscience, the one grounded in "freedom and justice for all."

Protest is the cry of the heart for the coming of the will of God.

To accept discrimination of any kind is to deny belief in the God of creation, the sacredness of the human contract, the commitment to the common good and the Constitution of the United States. If we really want to preserve this democracy, we must protest evil of every kind. To preserve the basic values we take for granted in these times, like those who preserved them before us, we Christians must have enough Christian conscience to do the same.

**SEPTEMBER 1** In a democracy, the greatest failure of them all is to take democracy for granted. Read, write, study, and participate in the public conversation.

**SEPTEMBER 2**  To protest evil is not a protest at all: it is a moral imperative.

**SEPTEMBER 3**  There are three virtues inherent in protest: We must commit ourselves to speaking up, speaking out, and speaking on until wrong is righted and the oppressed are free.

**SEPTEMBER 4**  One of religion's weaknesses is this: Too often it teaches us to be "nice," but it does not teach us to be good. We learn acceptance of suffering, but we do not learn that we have a responsibility to resist it.

**SEPTEMBER 5**  There is no such thing as being "neutral" when we are confronted with moral evil. As Archbishop Desmond Tutu from South Africa taught: "If an elephant has its foot on the tail of a mouse and you say that you are neutral, the mouse will not appreciate your neutrality."

**SEPTEMBER 6**  To be silent in the face of injustice is to be complicit. Silence means consent. As Elie Wiesel wrote, "We must take sides. Neutrality helps the oppressor, never the victim.

Silence encourages the tormentor, never the tormented."

**SEPTEMBER 7** Protesters who amplify their voices by joining like-minded groups make it impossible for evil to thrive underground. William Faulkner writes, "Never be afraid to raise your voice for honesty and truth and compassion against injustice and lying and greed. If people all over the world...would do this, it would change the earth."

**SEPTEMBER 8** "Nice" is when I refuse to participate in a public protest because "people would think I'm a radical." "Good" is when I do it because I'm not a radical but because I want my government to be what it says it is: just and equal and honest. "Protest beyond the law is not a departure from democracy," Howard Zinn wrote. "It is absolutely essential to it."

**SEPTEMBER 9** God created the world, but God did not finish it. That's our responsibility. What isn't done right here and now is our fault. Ours. No one else's. Good intentions and passive ignorance do not get us a pass.

**SEPTEMBER 10**   The world we leave to our children and grandchildren is toxic, fragile, and finite. They will live with the "sins of their parents" for generations to come. Most of all, they will know that we knew and did nothing: never wrote the governor a letter, never cast a vote to protest injustice, never joined a group working for change, never told a soul that we were against any single policy at all. (Now tell your children again how much you want them to have a good life.)

**SEPTEMBER 11**   To know, to protest, and to fail is not failure. To know but do nothing is a failure of soul. As Fred Shuttlesworth says, "Confrontation is not bad. Goodness is supposed to confront evil."

**SEPTEMBER 12**   Change does not happen at once. It takes time before everyone realizes that there's a problem. Then it takes more time to understand it. Finally, it takes a while before the world stands up and says, "Stop this." But someone has to stand up first or nothing will happen at all. Ever.

**SEPTEMBER 13** Whatever you're doing to bring justice as well as mercy, keep on doing it. Do it, even when it doesn't seem to work. Do it when it's long and hard and boring. As the Roman poet Ovid wrote, "Dripping water hollows out stone, not through force but through persistence."

**SEPTEMBER 14** Social change starts with personal change. Where are you on the continuum?

**SEPTEMBER 15** Beware the difference between "good" and what is done in the name of good. Air pollution done in the name of saving jobs is simply the first step toward the destruction of the planet. Then, no one will have a decent job. Marie von Ebner-Eschenbach writes, "There would be less evil on earth if evil could never be done in the name of good."

**SEPTEMBER 16** The quickest trip to evil is the road called "everybody's doing it" or "nobody else is complaining about it." Leo Tolstoy writes, "Wrong does not cease to be wrong because the majority share in it." Read and study and think....

**SEPTEMBER 17** To rebel out of love for something is not defiance. It is spiritual maturity.

**SEPTEMBER 18** It is so often easier to be wrong than it is to be different. But sometimes, to be good, it is necessary to be different in order not to be wrong. Franz Jägerstätter, for instance, refused to say, "Heil Hitler," the Nazi salute. His actions were more powerful than his words could ever have been.

**SEPTEMBER 19** Don't be afraid to speak, even alone. One sound in the midst of silence has the effect of a volcano. Anthony Marra says of it, "A single whisper can be quite a disturbance when the rest of the audience is silent."

**SEPTEMBER 20** To claim your voice when the world is silent about evil is not to be feared, not to be condemned, not to be criticized. After all, why else did God give us language at all? No other animal needs it.

**SEPTEMBER 21** It's not voice that is lacking when evil overcomes our little worlds. It is courage that is missing. The only question then is, What is it we are striving to maintain through silence that is more important than the quality of our souls?

**SEPTEMBER 22** The difference between holiness and indifference in times of moral pressure is the character we bring to the moment. Indifference assumes that silence will save it. Holiness knows that silence will sully it.

**SEPTEMBER 23** Aristotle teaches: "You will never do anything in this world without courage. It is the greatest quality of the mind next to honor." At the same time, courage is the muscle of the soul. It needs exercise to strengthen it. Be courageous once and the gospel will forever be safe with you.

**SEPTEMBER 24** Don't be afraid to be rejected. Be worried that your heart may be true to the voice of God but your courage too weak to sustain it. "Standing for right when it is unpopular," Margaret Chase Smith said, "is a true test of moral character."

**SEPTEMBER 25** Here's the kind of truth that will out in the end: History has taught that the first demonstration for women's suffrage in Pennsylvania was in Philadelphia. Except that's wrong. So even if you do not get the credit you deserve, be true to the good no matter who doesn't notice it.

**SEPTEMBER 26** We just learned that it was here, in Erie, Pennsylvania, my hometown, that the first public march for women's rights in Pennsylvania was held in 1913. We know that now because that story was just discovered by the local museum. Makes you wonder what other women's history-changing stories are buried in some obscure archives.

**SEPTEMBER 27** But the march for women in Erie, population about 40,000 then, also set the tone that women could identify with. It wasn't about defiance. They didn't go to the streets to simply get attention. They braved the disapproval both of men and of the church itself, for more important reasons than that. Augusta Fleming, president of the Northwestern Pennsylvania Equal Franchise Association and their leader that day, encouraged local women to participate in a pre-event newspaper interview: "Gain victory over fear and walk firm and erect."

**SEPTEMBER 28** Augusta Fleming also said, "Remember that you are only one in a great army—that you are marching for a principle—and that being government of the people, for the people and by the whole people. Your motive is unselfish. You are trying to gain citizenship that you may do your part to bring about better legislation for the protection of home, children and the weak." And so must we.

**SEPTEMBER 29** Never believe that protest is infidelity to anything. On the contrary, it exists to make a good thing better. As the philosopher Albert Camus writes: "Rebellion cannot exist without a strange form of love."

**SEPTEMBER 30** Ask yourself what you are protesting now. Nothing? In a day and age when we put immigrant children in cages?

Pile so many women/mothers in a cement floor room that none of them can lie down to sleep? Dismiss the trafficking of young girls as something they brought upon themselves as prostitutes? At the age of fourteen? And you are protesting nothing? May God forgive us all.

OCTOBER

# I Learned It While Fishing

I know there are two sides to the ecology argument. One group argues that every part of nature lives off of something else and so the destruction of another species is normal. The other group reminds me that we ourselves are just another species of animal life and should take care of it all. I am much closer to this group.

Question: Are we here to share the world or dominate it? Hmmmm.

Then I think of all those days spent fishing with my father.

"Jo," he said, "throw that fish back. It's too small to keep."

Pause.

"No, it isn't, Dad," I said. "I already measured it."

The look.

"Jo, inches have nothing to do with it. You are not fishing because without it you will have nothing to eat. We throw that fish back so that next year there will be enough for everyone to eat."

The fish, healthy, squirming, strong, went back into the water to spawn and multiply. Clearly, fishing was not simply about filling a stringer.

Fishing became for me, clearly a city kid, the lesson of a lifetime: what we do to nature—to water, to land, to animals, to trees, to streams—we do to ourselves. Most of all, if what we're doing changes life for this generation, it will certainly affect the next generation. One way or another.

Watching one part of nature after another dry up, die out, and turn to dust, we can see the future in front of us. We're not imagining things; we're watching it happen to our own land, our own beaches, our own clean water, our own gardens, our own forests and lowlands, our own vines and fishing grounds.

Whole species of animals are dying out or, in some cases, coming back to reclaim habitats long covered over with cement. So we're running them off again—without doing a thing to reserve enough land for them so that they can thrive too.

But none of those things are the real problem. The real problem is the lack of leadership in the country. Senators and representatives work day and night to win the next election and they do it best, apparently, by standing for nothing in the meantime.

We could mitigate the worst effects of the climate crisis if we had a Congress and a president that planned as much for the future of the entire country as they do for their own next election.

We could guarantee a healthy ecology tomorrow if we refused to vote for anyone who did not support science-based legislation to secure the kinds of harvest, homes, water, air, oceans, and trees earlier generations left to us.

You see, God created the world, but God did not complete it. That God left to us. Maybe we are seeing this era's original sin—its lack of impulse control, its disdain for humility—in centuries of overfishing writ large.

**OCTOBER 1** The world has been turned into steel and glass. We have to go on guided nature walks now to see what we're missing. Maybe that's why we no longer see the price we are paying for our own demise.

**OCTOBER 2** It's hard to teach anyone to want to preserve what we do not see and so do not value. Rachel Carson writes of it, "The more clearly we can focus our attention on the wonders and realities of the universe about us, the less taste we shall have for destruction."

**OCTOBER 3** We teach science and biology and nature studies in our schools, yes. But the question is, can we afford to wait until we have enough representatives and senators who have taken those courses to understand why they ought to be voting for them? Chris Maser writes, "What we are doing to the forests of the world is but a mirror reflection of what we are doing to ourselves and to one another."

**OCTOBER 4**  Our generation ushered in the war of the sexes and gave an entirely new meaning to the concept of "equality." What great new ideas of the soul is our generation addressing now? "Without a vision, the people perish," Scripture reminds us.

**OCTOBER 5**  What we teach children about the way to tend the earth, to protect the animals, to preserve the environment, will benefit them a great deal more than what they learn from playing violent video games.

**OCTOBER 6**  The new flight to nationalism is nothing more than the attempt of an older generation to maintain control of a computer-dependent, cosmological, ecological, and global world they know nothing about. It would be good to remember that the human quest for conquest ends only in the awareness of the need to conquer the arrogance of the self.

**OCTOBER 7**  Earlier generations knew two things: First, that young people had the energy it takes to build a society and secure a civilization. Second, that older people had the wisdom that years of experience bring to guide society and civilization through the dark spots of its development. Now we are struggling with the war between the generations. This generation grew up with computers, high-tech medicine, robotics, and computerized militarism. They define life very differently than older generations do. Wisdom has always been seen as the capstone of age. Now wisdom and knowledge are in contention. Is one possible without the other?

**OCTOBER 8**  Without both wisdom and knowledge, ideals and values, understanding of what's possible and a vision of what must be, we are all doomed to fail. As Gandhi put it, "Earth provides enough to satisfy everyone's needs but not everyone's greed."

**OCTOBER 9** Human community cannot be built on computers. Nevertheless, without computers global community can never really happen. So what is the solution? Community that is based on more than simple togetherness.

**OCTOBER 10** Transition from the industrial society to the technological society must depend on ideals and values if humanity is to be preserved as we move from the inadequacy of the present to the potential of the future. As Thomas Berry writes, "The natural world is the larger sacred community to which we belong.... To damage this community is to diminish our own existence."

**OCTOBER 11** The problem the world faces in a time of major transition is how to mobilize society to make both the physical and the spiritual moves that great change takes. To go from one kind of world to another means that we must revalue and reshape the way we think about everything. But that can be done only one person at a time. Which means that we must each do it consciously or risk the feeling of alienation such newness brings.

**OCTOBER 12** The important thing at a time of social change is to make ourselves part of the change. The new ecological perspective is not done as a nation. It can be done only one person at a time. You and me. Jane Goodall tells us how when she says: "You cannot get through a single day without having an impact on the world around you. What you do makes a difference, and you have to decide what kind of difference you want to make."

**OCTOBER 13** To live in rhythm with the seasons was natural in an agricultural society. Now in the technological age, it has become a spiritual discipline, a sign of maturity yet to be developed.

**OCTOBER 14** Nature is the part of us an urban world is missing. For it we have substituted crowds, noise, and perpetual motion. Was it worth it?

**OCTOBER 15** To live with nature as an enemy is to fail life. To walk through nature as its dictator is to wrench the balance of life. To fail to see the voice of God in the balance of nature, the struggles of nature, is to go through life blind of heart and deaf of soul.

**OCTOBER 16** To be a contemplative now it is necessary to walk through nature softly, to be in tune with the rhythm of life, to learn from the cycles of time, to listen to the heartbeat of the universe, to love nature, to protect nature, and to discover in nature the presence and the power of God.

**OCTOBER 17** To be really dedicated to God, we must be dedicated to the whole of creation.

**OCTOBER 18** We need to understand that what we do to nature, we do to ourselves. But there is not a chance that we will stop clogging the air with pollution, the seas with garbage, and the land with chemicals until it hurts us. Not a chance, that is, until the pollution makes breathing impossible, the fish sick, and the vegetables full of poison.

**OCTOBER 19** We recycle a little. We sign a petition or two. We wait for someone else to do something. And if you're concerned about the impact of refugees on our own resources and still say little or nothing about the climate crisis, you haven't seen anything yet. This ecological crisis is driving the largest global refugee migration in history. The world is turning upside down and we go blithely on.

**OCTOBER 20** How is it that we can ignore nature as the eleventh commandment, as a deeply moral obligation of a Christian? God made us, we say, "to know, to love, and to serve" the God of creation with all our heart. We were taught that sex was a sin, lying and stealing were sins, missing Mass was a sin. But destroying creation? Oh, please....

**OCTOBER 21** So, the overfishing goes on. Tuna and whale populations are getting smaller while the price of them increases as a result. The air pollution and water pollution and land pollution go on whatever the effect on small children and asthmatics, the elderly and the malnourished.

**OCTOBER 22** If what we're doing does not change life much for this generation it will certainly affect the next generation. One way or another. Then whose sin will it be: theirs or ours?

**OCTOBER 23** We all believe these things, of course, so what's missing in our national commitment? This, perhaps. As Robert Swan says, "The greatest threat to our planet is the belief that someone else will save it."

**OCTOBER 24** The only calculation that's missing is this one: How many cities will have to flood before we demand that our government meet its responsibility more to the future than to its present profits? As Wangari Maathai warned us, "The generation that destroys the environment is not the generation that pays the price."

**OCTOBER 25** How is it that our conception of morality has so easily ignored our relationship to nature? "No one," Marguerite of Navarre said, "ever perfectly loved God who did not perfectly love God's creatures in this world."

**OCTOBER 26** Theology is clear: We are here to develop and preserve what God created for the sake of all. Destruction and domination, it is clear, simply cannot do that.

**OCTOBER 27** The greatest war we are facing at the present time is the war within ourselves: Shall we destroy the planet or shall we defend it?

**OCTOBER 28** To be in a city does not forgive us our Christian commitment to creation. "Nature," Gary Snyder writes, "is not a place to visit. It is home."

**OCTOBER 29** Remember always that there are those who are vested in keeping things as they are. Which, of course, is why we didn't have electric cars thirty years ago. Think about that before you vote.

**OCTOBER 30** "Where is God?" the catechism asked. "God is everywhere," the catechism answered. The answer is often ignored, but the answer, if God is really God, is certainly true. God is the stuff of the universe. In everything created resides the energy, the life, the image, the nature of the Creator.

**OCTOBER 31** "The truly holy person welcomes all that is earthly," Hildegard of Bingen writes. And then she goes on, "Glance at the sun. See the moon and the stars. Gaze at the beauty of earth's greenings. Now, think. What delight God gives to humankind with all these things. All nature is at the disposal of humankind. We are to work with it. For without it we cannot survive."

# Why Write? Why Read?

By way of explanation: If anyone cares, I carry within me quotations from Scripture, great literature, stunning poetry, and sacred reading, for almost every occasion in life. They form a pathway of pillars that steady me through all the shaky moments of human growth. They make every day a new reflection on life and alert me to my own immersion in it.

I collect bits and pieces of thought from every possible level of great writing:

Like Aristotle's insight, for instance, "Knowing yourself is the beginning of all wisdom."

Or Einstein's statement that "Any fool can know. The point is to understand."

Or the line from the biblical story of the good Samaritan that reads, "First the priest (the professional religious) passed the wounded man by, then the scribe (the holy layman) hurried by him. But then along came the Samaritan (the social, religious outcast) who picked the man up and got him the help he needed."

The idea that no help was provided for the needy by those who called themselves "religious" affected me deeply. The stark simplicity of the statement opened my eyes to insights that deserved more thought. It made me aware in a new way of what, down deep, I had always taken for granted.

Awareness is the gift of great writers to those who would come after them. Writers we never meet nevertheless become our companions on the journey of life. The insights of good writers become beacons to their readers. I collect them in great numbers.

But don't be fooled: Writing is not really about words at all, beautiful as they may be, elegant as they may seem, demanding as the writer's talent is in capturing our attention. No amount of words without meaning, no number of details without the power to stretch our worldview, our sensitivities, can really be called "writing."

No, writing is about ideas.

It's about what's inside a writer, not simply what one person may read of another person's musings. It's about what's rumbling around in the writer's soul that stretches our own. Most of all, it's the writer's sharing of their own personal insights that seed in a reader a whole new consciousness of what it really means to be alive.

The simple record of an experience is not what makes for great writing. The log of a person's trip up a mountain, for instance, may be interesting but not necessarily soul-shaping. It is the distillation of the climber's experiences that brings us to confront our own understandings, to examine their depth, to challenge their quality and caliber. It's the writer who opens our minds to hear the heartbeat of the world that makes writing the sacrament of insight.

Then, when we ourselves come to that moment on the mountain of life that demands all our attention, requires all our strength, confronts all our own expectations, we find in ourselves an icon to guide us.

What good writers bring to the exposure of the mundane grows us all, enables us all to see our own world differently. They lead us down new paths of thought, open up new possibilities, and challenge what we have too easily taken for granted.

It is, in other words, finding the writer who opens us to the great insights of life, who opens us to ourselves, and stretches us beyond data to meaning.

Good writing demands good readers. Great personal growth requires the inquiring mind.

All religious traditions, therefore, call for serious personal attention to the great wisdom of the past, the writings that have lasted through time, that is borne from the heart of one generation to another through the discipline of sacred reading.

**NOVEMBER 1** The modern world is a cascade of ideas coming at us from every direction: Twitter, TV, in a frenzy of images, words. Discovering how to unmask the impact of them makes for the true intellectual.

**NOVEMBER 2** Writers change the world by requiring readers to rethink what, until the casting of such sentences, had been accepted without scrutiny. Not to become a good reader allows everyone else to do our thinking for us.

**NOVEMBER 3** Writing is the surgery of the soul. It opens us to criticism; it makes better thinkers of us. It releases in us our own most careful critics.

**NOVEMBER 4** Writing is only one-half of the human communication system. The work of the writer is not really finished until readers probe its inner core, squeeze the juice out of it, begin to see differently than they did before they read it.

**NOVEMBER 5** Writing is what lets the steam out of the human heart. It exposes us to the emotional underbelly of the human being. It opens us to ourselves. "Knowledge," Carl Jung writes, "rests not upon truth alone, but upon error also."

**NOVEMBER 6** Journaling our feelings is another whole way of going through life, it gives us the opportunity to examine them. Otherwise, they may consume us to the point that we forget the situations that spawned them. Then, unchallenged, the heat of them can live on in us untamed.

**NOVEMBER 7** Learning to mine the words that matter—like "faith," or "love," or "anger," perhaps—we go one depth deeper into our own souls. We discover what we really mean—or don't mean at all—in using them. Then, we are ready to begin the spiritual exploration of ourselves.

**NOVEMBER 8** *Lectio Divina*, the slow and thoughtful reading of a word, a phrase, a sentence of Scripture, for instance, is an invitation to a contemplative way of life. It makes us seeders of our hearts and minds with new life. It puts life under the magnifying glass of the soul.

**NOVEMBER 9** The pursuit of the right word rather than merely being satisfied with a trite word makes us razor-sharp thinkers. It also makes us the kind of writers that shock the world into new consciousness.

**NOVEMBER 10** To be a good reader is every bit as important as being a good writer. The good reader wrestles an idea to the ground in an attempt to understand what the writer is really saying. The good reader begins an internal dialogue with an equally good writer.

**NOVEMBER 11** It is in writing that we come to know ourselves. It's there that we can plot the future and examine the past for its learnings, its warnings, and its pitfalls. As Eric Hoffer says, "Many of the insights of the saints stem from their experience as sinners."

**NOVEMBER 12** If we can bear to write our ideas down, we can learn from them. As long as we are willing to take them up, read them again, and look at them square on, they lie there waiting for us, not to justify them but to redeem them for the future. As Aristotle wrote, "Knowing yourself is the beginning of wisdom."

**NOVEMBER 13** Every book we read is a potential mentor. Gather them carefully. Read them continually. Then, the learnings of others and the insights from the past can light the way to our own future.

**NOVEMBER 14** Every good book we read stretches our thinking to another level of human development. It is the equivalent of the harvest of the fruits of life.

**NOVEMBER 15** The reality of the present: we have bowdlerized language into emojis and contractions. Where shall we go to stretch the literary mind now?

**NOVEMBER 16**  Good writers do not so much give us data as they give us a model of how to use the insights that data brings. One person sees the rising temperature of the earth as a sign of lengthening summers and longer days at the beach. Another sees it as a crisis, warning against careless living, about human self-centeredness. As Malcolm Forbes wrote, "The best vision is insight."

**NOVEMBER 17**  As we grow we learn that ignorance is our greatest internal enemy. But it is writers who make us learners all our lives. They set out to awaken the rest of the world to situations that, without them, we would either ignore or deny.

**NOVEMBER 18**  Writers save us from isolation, from the corruption of invincibility. They set out to help people understand what they are too busy to study for themselves. They allow us to live in two worlds at once: our own private one and the larger world of the human community for whom we are also, like the good Samaritan, responsible.

**NOVEMBER 19**  The great power of good writing is that the answers to life's questions lie in multiple genres just waiting for us to find the format that fits us best, that affects us most deeply: essays, poetry, drama, and fiction. Like all our best friends, they call to different parts of us in different ways to make us better.

**NOVEMBER 20**  Writing and its various genres give us entrée to ideas from every perspective, from serious thought to heartrending poetry. They each wait to take us into places and moments we would never see without them.

**NOVEMBER 21**  Writers make doubt and uncertainty one of the great gifts of life. They lead us on beyond ourselves to the rest and the best of the world. "Doubt," the philosopher René Descartes wrote, "is the origin of wisdom."

**NOVEMBER 22**  Writing is not meant to enable us to wile our lives away superficially, uselessly. Writing is meant to bring the many layers of life to us so that we don't have to live every one of them ourselves in order to grow to our fullest emotional self.

**NOVEMBER 23** Not everyone can speak multiple languages, as important as that gift may be. But everyone who reads deeply and regularly can learn what it means to look at life from multiple directions. The Zen Master teaches: A scholar was bragging to a boatman about all the knowledge he had acquired. "Can you swim?" the boatman asked. "No," the scholar replied. "Then all your knowledge is wasted," the boatman said, "because this boat is sinking."

**NOVEMBER 24** It is great writing that keeps us learning from early on until the very end of life. By taking us into the experiences and insights of others it culls and shapes our own.

**NOVEMBER 25** Thanks to writers who welcome us into their lives and thoughts, we find another path to growth. By wrestling with their experiences and insights, we have a chance to become wise ourselves. As Doug Larson puts it, "Wisdom is the reward you get for a lifetime of listening when you'd have preferred to talk."

**NOVEMBER 26** Years of study provide us with the knowledge we need to compare one kind of data with another. Reading provides us with the opportunity to feel the feelings of others, to understand situations other than our own, to distinguish between data and insight.

**NOVEMBER 27** To read great literature is to see life and history and emotional development one piece, one person at a time. In each of them then, we have the opportunity to consider how developed we may yet be ourselves. As Samuel Johnson said, "A writer only begins a book. A reader finishes it."

**NOVEMBER 28** Reading allows us to observe someone else's life or ideas or feelings without being seen. That way, unlike in our own lives, we can pause to consider whether what we are seeing is what we would also like to see in ourselves. Author Joyce Carol Oates says of it, "Reading is the sole means by which we slip, involuntarily, often helplessly, into another's skin, another's voice, another's soul."

**NOVEMBER 29** Writers are the wisdom figures, the spiritual directors of our lives. We must choose them carefully for fear we may stay only on our own level rather than reach always for a stage of soul higher than we are at present. Wendell Berry says of it, "It is not from ourselves that we learn to be better than we are."

**NOVEMBER 30** Great writing enables writers to speak new truths boldly and old truths newly. At the same time, great writing enables readers to see life through eyes other than their own. Both are changed by the process.

# The Feast of New Life

It isn't the strings of lights, warming as they are. It isn't the bells that make the season beautiful, however entrancing their magnetic call. It isn't the tree and all the memories it conjures up of love and harmony that makes our image of Christmas complete. No, Christmas is not only more than those things; it is completely other than those things. Christmas is our image of life at its best. It is the symbol of the eternal giving of the self.

It is about a baby born into innocence who became a model of standing up for those for whom no one else stood at all: the needy, the fringe, the strangers, the women. This one stood up against the fraudsters and the hypocrites, the ones who draped themselves in the mantle of holiness but distorted the meaning of the laws they imposed on everyone else.

Indeed, Christmas is the call not simply to give things to others but to give ourselves to everyone all the rest of the year.

So, string the lights and follow the glow of them to those in need of you. Ring the bells and let their beauty draw you into the glorious rhythm that makes giving, giving, giving possible. Most of all, plant a tree yourself as a sign of your commitment to the growth of the earth.

**DECEMBER 1** Christmas is the feast of new birth, of beginning again to make our lives full of hope and possibility. It is the very feast of God's goodness and the belief that we not only want the best for everyone but also do the best for everyone.

**DECEMBER 2** The sight of a newborn baby, the very icon of Christmas, reminds us all that there is meant to be in us yet, the desire to start over, to do it right, to be all that we can be. We are not born finished; we are born to become all that we can be: good, kind, giving.

**DECEMBER 3** When Christmas gets lost in the trappings of the commercial world, the Child Jesus reveals to us its pure purpose. Born naked, just like he was, we too are meant "to grow in wisdom and age and grace." Every year the gift from God to us is the time and the will to do just that.

**DECEMBER 4** Jesus too was born poor. A carpenter's son, he worked hard just to live a decent life. But most of all, he had learned to hold others up along the way. He taught us, standing here under all the lights in the midst of all the wrapping paper, that life's real gifts lie elsewhere.

**DECEMBER 5** Life is a great gift. It must be invested in something that doubles its possibility. We must set out to grow its gifts. We must work to reap everything that life has to give. And we must do these things, not for our sake alone but to bring God's will for everyone else also to fullness.

**DECEMBER 6** Too many who receive God's gift of life deny its purpose and its gifts in themselves. Too often we fail to understand that the gifts God has given us have been given for us to give away to others. How sad. Danny Kaye wrote once, "Life is a great big canvas; throw all the paint on it you can." Do not overlook the gifts of God in you and around you—ever.

**DECEMBER 7** Overcoming the fear of life and its failures is the greatest gift of all. But failure is not failure if in the end we succeed despite it. The call of God is to go on just when we think we can't try again. "Either you decide to stay in the shallow end of the pool or you go out into the ocean," said Christopher Reeve. And who besides actor and quadriplegic Christopher Reeve was greater proof to us than that?

**DECEMBER 8** Beware the day you say of yourself, "If only I had done that and not this,..." Lament is not an excuse for not starting again. It is simply proof that we have learned one more thing about life on the way.

**DECEMBER 9** What is left in you to be done must be sought after. It is God's call within you to the more of you. It may not end the way you hoped, but it will end in the lesson of your life. George

Eliot writes of it, "It's never too late to be who you might have been."

**DECEMBER 10**  We must remember about life and the beckoning to it that Christmas brings that it's not others who obstruct it. It is only that they are struggling toward their own hopes as they go. Smile at them and go on. Ian Maclaren taught it over a century ago, "Be kind, for everyone you meet is fighting a hard battle." Help them along and your journey will be easier too.

**DECEMBER 11**  When the Christmas lights go on, we begin to see another, brighter world. Why? Because then we remember that the light of Christ goes before us to lead the way. Our small lives become lit with the joy of it which, too often, we allow ourselves to forget.

**DECEMBER 12**  What the crib confronts us with every Christmas is the challenge to go into new things open, vulnerable, willing, and trusting. In the end, those may be the very qualities that separate the happy from the unhappy.

**DECEMBER 13** Our life can seem as barren sometimes as it must have seemed for Jesus, Mary, and Joseph in a strange land and an animal byre. But we all wind up where we're meant to be. There is something for us to do here. Something for us to learn here. Take it as gift. "A moment's insight," Oliver Wendell Holmes Sr. wrote, "is sometimes worth a life's experience."

**DECEMBER 14** However much we love the lights and bells and songs of Christmas, we know down deep that they will not last. Which is nothing more than a good dose of reality. But then it is imperative to remember that Christmas does come to everyone at some time. For as Arthur Rubinstein says, "I have found that if you love life, life will love you back."

**DECEMBER 15** As you mark the Christmas holidays with the children in your life, remember the Chinese proverb God wants us to know: "A child's life is like a piece of paper on which every person leaves a mark." Then, make sure that the marks of your own life can bring the best out of theirs.

**DECEMBER 16**  It's easy to forget that Christmas joy is meant to refresh us as we ourselves go on through life with all its dullness, duties, and dry, dry days. But those dry days are not useless. On the contrary, they demand the best of us. They demand that we rekindle a spark of Christmas joy in us so that every person we touch goes away happier than they were before. Florence Shinn says it best, perhaps, "The game of life is the game of boomerangs. Our thoughts, deeds, and words return to us sooner or later, with astounding accuracy."

**DECEMBER 17**  We are each a step in someone else's life. Be true to the will of God for them. Give them the kind of understanding that you have been given, and then allow them to find that truth on their own, which is, of course, the greatest gift of all. Jeannette Rankin says of them, "You take people as far as they will go, not as far as you would like them to go."

**DECEMBER 18** Christmas is the morning when we all remember what life has been created for: the joy of living it, the sense of achievement that comes with doing it well, the awareness that great delight comes out of darkness if we give ourselves to the mystery of it.

**DECEMBER 19** When you are tempted to think that your life has been for nothing, there is an easy criterion to use: How have you been to others? That, of course, is the only real gift you have to give them. Or to put it another way, Isiah Thomas, the professional basketball player, says, "If all I'm remembered for is being a good basketball player, then I've done a bad job with the rest of my life."

**DECEMBER 20** The great Christmas question is, how many years does it take to discover that life is not about "success"? Life is simply and only about growing up myself and then, when I'm really a spiritual adult, taking care of everybody else. Anna Quindlen reminds us, "The thing that is really hard, and really amazing, is giving up on being perfect and beginning the work of becoming yourself."

Each Christmas gives us another point at which we review what we wanted to become in life as compared to what we have become: wealthy and kind; cold-hearted and poor; open and growing, or closed-minded and afraid. "Change your thoughts and you change the world," Norman Vincent Peale wrote. Think about it.

Christmas has so much to tell us about ourselves: annoyed or happy, disgusted or loving, money-centered or family-centered, irritated or spiritually challenged. And why? Because one of those choices is eternal. The other one will only make time harder than ever. Christmas is the time to take stock—or another year on the edge of our lives will be lost. As Cora L.V. Hatch writes, "We cannot direct the wind, but we can adjust the sails."

**DECEMBER 23**  All creation teaches us that life is one new beginning after another, one tree downed and one tree seeded after another, one flower picked and one flower planted after another. It is having the courage to end what is finished, to begin what is fragile that is the measure of life well lived.

**DECEMBER 24**  Jesus is born. Jesus is born an infant, just like you and me. Jesus is born with a future to shape and a life to measure. Maybe this Christmas is just the time to review your life—when there is still a chance to change its final stamp.

**DECEMBER 25**  It is in the light of the stable and the sight of the child that we realize for what we must spend our efforts in this warring, confused, exploitative world: Whatever we have done or hope to do, we must make this world better. For all of them, the infants of the poor and powerless as well as of the rich and the royalty.

**DECEMBER 26** We have nothing to do with our births and little to do with our deaths. It is only what separates the two over which we have any control at all. We can live it or we can simply wait for it to go by.

**DECEMBER 27** We are the masters of our souls. We can make the present full of character whatever the cost. What more can there possibly be about a life well lived?

**DECEMBER 28** Don't worry about living a long life, however delightful that may seem. We are here, like the child in the stable, to be able to answer one question and one question only. And that question is a simple one: What was my life lived for?

**DECEMBER 29** Your life is your greatest gift. Make it your legacy, not your waste. As Gilda Radner said, "While we have the gift of life, it seems to me the only tragedy is to allow part of us to die—whether it is our spirit, our creativity, or our glorious uniqueness."

**DECEMBER 30** Go through all the Christmas and New Year rituals again, of course. But this time remember what they are giving back and demanding from you.

**DECEMBER 31** Now set out to make life next year even more loving, more lit up with hope, more ringing with joy. "The bitterest tears shed over graves," Harriet Beecher Stowe wrote, "are for words left unsaid and deeds left undone." Tell someone you haven't spoken to for years, "Merry Christmas," and to someone who needs what you will give them, "Happy New Year."

In this ground-breaking book, ten young women active in ministry share their thoughts, aspirations, questions, and desires with Sister Joan Chittister. The conversations unfold in a series of letters. Each letter writer shares an experience from her life or ministry, and Joan then responds with affirmation and challenge, sharing her wisdom, inspiration and courage with those vitally committed to the church.

144 PAGES | $18.95 | 5½" X 8½" | 9781627854863